THE 7 PILLARS OF
CRYSTAL
HEALING

63 Techniques & Strategies to **Transform** Your Health With
the **Power of Stone Magic.** Have a More Balanced Life
by Protecting Your Energy. Gem Remedies for 50+ Symptoms

MONIQUE WAGNER

Table of Contents

Introduction

If you're like most spiritual people, you've probably felt a strong connection between your mind, body, and the world around you. You're not the only one. Many other people throughout history have noticed this. What you are feeling is the inherent interconnectedness of the universe and everything in it. Forces we cannot even fathom are at work in our world, shaping our every move and thought. These are not scary or chaotic forces, though. Some might be, but most work to bring the universe into balance; restoring the inherent harmony at the core of our world is their mission. If we can harness these forces, or at least understand them, then we can start building a more connected and balanced life that is as in sync with the universe as possible.

You might find that this feeling waxes or wanes during particularly difficult phases of your life. This is your natural forces attempting to realign themselves during a transition. On one hand, trials in your life might cause you to want to turn away from the universe and its forces. On the other hand, they might want you to turn toward them more than ever. This is the right path. When dealing with the powerful forces of the universe, we want to be as much on their side as possible, working in tandem with them rather than against them. There is a lot to be gained from harnessing the universe's power, especially during difficult periods of your life. Connecting with these powers can help us understand what the universe might be trying to tell us through our hard times and will help us manifest the kind of life we want instead. If you are struggling, feeling like you just can't get ahead in the world no matter how hard you try, you should know that there are ways to make the universe work for you instead of the other way around.

So, what are these mysterious methods for learning about and manipulating the universe? Well, there are learning methods, like Tarot and astrology, which help you chart the course of your life and understand where your destiny and temperament come from. But if you want to have control over your life through mystical means, then crystals are the best way to go about that. Crystals and crystal healing have been around for literally thousands of years. They began in Ancient India and have continued to grow and evolve in their practice over time, eventually culminating in the modern practice we know today. Crystals all have unique mineral properties that can help link us with spiritual forces and attempt to guide those forces to help us. Crystals can aid in a number of life's problems, helping you with almost any facet of life from money to relationships to career goals. Making a serious change to your life by using crystals is possible and has been done throughout all of human history, making it a tried and true practice.

In this book, I will share with you the seven basic pillars of crystals and crystal healing. We will look at each of the fundamental qualities of crystals to help you get started on your crystal journey. Over the course of this book, you will learn how forces like vibrations can shape you, the people around you, and the universe as a whole. You will find 63 techniques, tips, and strategies to help you transform your health and find inner peace. These techniques, tips, and strategies are peppered throughout the entire book. And it's intentionally designed this way to serve as your guide along each step of the process.

You will learn to harness these vibrations with crystals. I will also teach you about the many different kinds of crystals, what they do, and the effects they can have on different areas of your life. There are hundreds of different kinds of crystals and a myriad of different ways you can use each of them, so the world of crystal practice is vast and anything but simple. After reading this book, you should have a good idea of how to choose the right crystals to achieve the results you are looking for in your life.

There was a time in my life when I felt lost and out of control. I felt that there were forces flying around me that were wreaking havoc in my life, yet I didn't know how to tame them. I was inspired by my Scandinavian neo-pagan roots to look into different spiritual practices to try and solve these deep problems I was grappling with in my life. I did my research and came to crystal healing. The more I learned about crystals, the more I realized that they could help me. I read up on many different kinds and began incorporating them into my everyday life, using them to correct a negative wavelength in my life or to manifest the things I had secretly dreamed of but was always too afraid to pursue. To my delight, I began to see amazing results. I am proud to say that I am no longer a sufferer of burnout and now feel that I have truly realigned myself through crystal healing to be the best person that I can possibly be. By writing this book, I want to help you discover the power of crystals and learn how to implement them to improve your life as I have improved mine.

This book takes a powerful but practical approach to crystal healing. I will be going through the seven pillars in a linear fashion so that you can ease into the process of crystal healing little by little. The first pillar will deal with the fundamentals of crystals. This is the section where I will give you an overview of the history of crystals as well as some of their most important applications and cross sections. Pillar 2 is where I will start to get into the practical aspects of crystals. Here, I will give you crucial information on which crystals you should buy and where you can buy them as well as some important classifications within the crystal family. In the third pillar, I will start to talk about some of the applications crystals can have in your life. In this section, we look at how you can use crystals and what they can help you with. After that, in the fourth pillar, we will step back and I'll guide you on how to prepare for a crystal session. This involves priming your crystals for practice and taking good care of them. Along the same lines, the fifth pillar will deal with storing and caring for your crystals, especially when you are not actively using them. The magic doesn't go away when you do, so you have to be very careful with dormant crystals and where and how you store them. In Pillar 6, I will give you a list of some of the most common types of crystals and how they can be used. Here, you will get an at-a-glance look at many different types to decide which ones you want to use for your own practice. And finally, in Pillar 7 we will deal specifically with the healing aspect of crystals, and I will show you how to use them to promote healing in your life and those of others. Through these seven pillars, you will learn the ins and outs of crystal healing, gaining new knowledge of a practice that can have a profound effect on your life and your relationship with the universe.

Pillar 1:
Fundamentals

Crystal healing is for everybody. It is one of the most common and ancient spiritual practices in the world, but what is it exactly, and how can we use it? You are probably curious about all the different things crystals can do as well as how they connect to other spiritual practices. In this pillar, I will be giving you a basic breakdown of crystals and all the things they can do. First, in Chapter 1, we will look at the definition and origins of crystal healing. This is the chapter where I will really lay down the foundation of what we call crystals. Then, in Chapter 2, we will examine the relationship between crystals and energy, investigating how crystals carry energy and what that energy might entail. Following that, Chapter 3 will deal with the relationship between crystals and chakras, another important spiritual practice that also originated in Ancient India. Chakras are very important to the energy and alignment of the body, so they have a very close connection to crystals. Finally, in Chapter 4 the last fundamental we will be examining is the connection between crystals and auras, which are also very important to current and ancient spiritual practices. Through these four chapters, I will give you a clear explanation of the basics of crystals so you can then move forward with acquiring them for yourself.

Chapter 1:
What Is Crystal Healing?

E ssentially, the process of crystal healing is to utilize the energy of certain crystals in order to have an effect on the body. Crystal healers and users believe that each crystal has a unique set of powers that are stored deep in its geological core. These crystals naturally hold this power but can be used by people to channel that power toward all sorts of things. You can thus select certain crystals based on their properties and attempt to channel them into the kind of healing you want to practice. This is the basic format for crystal healing, but the actual practice is much wider and deeper. Since crystal healing has been practiced for much of human history all over the globe and still continues strongly to this day, there are many different schools of thought and cultural practices that use different methods of crystal healing simultaneously. There are also many different aspects of crystal healing, even within certain practices. You can wear crystals on your body, use them in tandem with meditation or massage, or incorporate them into certain rituals. Crystals can also be used in medicinal practices, psychological healing, and to help repair relationships. In this chapter, we will look at some of the fundamental aspects of crystal healing, helping you to understand where crystals came from, what they can do, and how you can use them in your spiritual practice.

History of Crystal Healing

Crystals have a rich history stretching back at least 6,000 years. It's hard to pin down exactly where the use of crystals started because there were simultaneous origins all over the world; however, we will focus on the three main traditions that got crystals going: Native American, South Asian, and European. These three cultures form the backbone of modern crystal practice, having each developed core concepts and distinct practices around the concept of crystal healing. In this section, I will give you a brief overview of how each of these cultures formed their understanding of crystal power.

Native American Crystal Practice

In America, crystal healing was practiced in particular by the Cherokee and Apache nations. The traditions were very standardized within these cultures and were taught explicitly through generations using a consistent methodology, yet they also evolved over time. Cherokee and Apache practices emphasize the core concepts of meditation and respect. These two aspects of crystal healing show great weight given to the power of crystals, emphasizing their evident importance. When handling crystals, according to the Cherokee and Apache nations, you must think about channeling your desires very carefully and clearly and treat them as though they are extremely powerful objects by showing them great respect. Looking at this practice, we can see where our current concepts around clarity of mind and respect for crystals come from.

South Asian Crystal Practice

On the Indian subcontinent, a crystal tradition was also brewing. In this part of the world, crystals were invariably tied to their main religion, Hinduism. Hinduism is one of the oldest currently practiced religions and is still the dominant official religion of India. In Hindu texts, called the Vedas, crystals came from the body of the demon Vala, thus harnessing his power within their materiality. This perspective on crystals emphasizes their intense power, being literally divine in their makeup, as well as their potential for evil. If you do not channel your crystals properly, they have the potential to bring chaos and destruction. All the more reason to treat your crystals with care and respect.

European Crystal Practice

In Europe, many pre-Christian cultures developed a crystal practice as well. Britain in particular has a rich history with crystals. In Western crystal practice, crystals are very closely related to the stars, particularly in astrology. Crystals were assigned meaning based on their associations with astrological signs, thus linking them with the mystery and power of the heavens. One unique aspect of European crystal practice is that, because of their link with natal astrology, people had certain crystals that they were particularly connected with. Your sun sign in astrology might relate to a certain crystal, which means that you would use that type of crystal if you were sick or needed help in some way. This system of having "patron crystals" is a particularly European invention, which later came to relate to the concept of patron saints. In this practice, we can see how individual identity and astrology were closely related to crystal practice.

Benefits of Crystals

So, now that you understand what crystals are and where they come from, you probably want to know what they can actually do for you. There are many ways crystals can benefit you. The benefits of crystals are generally divided into three main groups: physical health, mental health, and manifestation. Here, we will give you a short description of these three categories of crystal benefits and how you can harness them.

Physical Health

There are many people who feel left behind by the modern medical world. Either because they have a chronic illness that they just can't get a diagnosis for, or maybe because they're a woman and feel that medical science doesn't care about the female body, or even simply because it is prohibitively expensive. For these reasons, many people are turning to alternative forms of medicine to feel more heard and to seek additional treatments not traditionally practiced by Western doctors. Though you should never take your health care completely into your own hands, especially if you have a life-threatening disease like cancer, you can supplement your existing medical treatment with crystals. For those with less life-threatening ailments, crystals are suitable. Crystals can also be a great form of alternative medicine for illnesses that don't have discovered causes or treatments within the medical community, such as migraines or chronic fatigue. Many people who experience these conditions feel left behind by the medical world and have found a lot of healing using crystal practices. They can help to align your energies and soothe the body to harness its natural immune responses, among other things. If you are suffering in a way that doctors just don't seem to be able to cure, then it's worth giving crystals a try.

Mental Health

An even more complicated component of the medical world is mental health care. Many people feel at the end of their rope when it comes to getting care for their mental health. They feel that they are dismissed, pigeonholed by rigid diagnoses, or overly medicated without much concern for individual needs. Crystals will help you ground yourself and forge a stronger connection with the earth and the universe around you, which can do wonders for your mental health. If you feel like your mental health issues are not being adequately addressed with modern psychology and nothing seems to work, then crystals can be a great thing to try.

Manifestation

Finally, you can use crystals even if you are not particularly suffering or if your problems are more external. Because crystals have such a strong power and connection to the universe, you can use them to make things happen outside your own body. Many people use crystals to help them with things like their careers, relationships, family, and even creativity. If you are looking for some answers that lie outside of yourself—in your destiny or your relationships with other people or the world at large—then you can definitely use crystals to try and bring a little more order to your life.

Difference Between Crystals and Gems

You might be wondering whether crystals are always the same as gems. After all, we use crystals in non-spiritualist jewelry on occasion alongside gems, so it can be hard sometimes for people to tell the difference between them. While there is some overlap between gems and crystals, they are not necessarily the same. Gems are mainly categorized by their purity. When you see something like a sapphire or diamond, they are usually ones that have been found to have a high purity of chemical makeup and thus will be cut and sold for value. Crystals, on the other hand, are not valued or even categorized by purity, but instead by their chemical shape. There is no inherently more "pure" crystal because they are just categorized by their material properties. A crystal also doesn't need to be shiny or reflective like a gem. Many crystals resemble rocks, completely opaque and hard. The final distinction, of course, is that crystals have spiritual properties and are used for healing purposes. Gems are not necessarily used for this purpose, so I won't be talking about them in this book. Now that you are familiar with the basic essentials of crystal healing, we can start to look at some of the things crystals interact with. In the next three chapters, we will be exploring the relationships crystals have with things like life energy, chakras, and auras.

Chapter 2:
Crystals and Energy

In the world of crystals, there are several cornerstone concepts at the core of the practice, one of which is the concept of energy. In crystal theology, each crystal has a particular energy that will help you harness that particular aspect of crystal power. When crystal healers are selecting a crystal, they will be using these energy concepts in order to choose which crystal is right for the occasion. If you choose the wrong crystal for your practice, then you will likely have a much harder time attaining the results you want. For this reason, you should educate yourself well on the concepts of crystal energy before you attempt your crystal practice. In this chapter, we will look at a few different aspects and applications of crystal energy to further your understanding of how crystals interact with our inherent spiritual sides.

Body Energy

The concept of crystal energy would not be complete if we did not address the energies that humans give off as well. In fact, everything in the universe is vibrating at a particular frequency. All these frequencies have to do with forces like heat, electricity, and chemical makeup. All humans vibrate at a particular frequency which denotes their specific energy. Have you ever noticed that certain people have "higher" energies than others or that certain people are more exhausting to be around than others? This is directly related to that person's energy. Just as crystals do, every person has their own particular energy that they give off. Moreover, humans also have different sections of our bodies that give off different frequencies than others. Many things might affect our energies in different parts of our bodies, such as relationships, stress, or even health problems.

When we are experiencing these misalignments in our body's energy, we can use crystals to rearrange our energies and try to bring them to a more balanced state. This is why people use crystals to heal their bodies and minds through energy and vibrations. So, for example, if you are vibrating at a lower frequency because of something in your life, you can use high-vibration crystals in order to bring balance back into your body through osmosis. Similarly, you can use crystals with lower vibrations to absorb some of the higher energy in your body and help you to get your energies lowered again. This is a fairly basic explanation with simply positive and negative values, but it gets the general concept across. In reality, there is a whole rainbow of energies that your body can be experiencing, with specialized crystals acting as a balancing agent for all your body's misalignments. In short, crystals help to regulate your energy with their own.

Stone Vibrations and Power

The idea that crystals vibrate is not a purely spiritual concept. In fact, crystal vibrations are a well-documented scientific phenomenon. In fact, crystal vibrations actually have the power to run small mechanical devices. For example, quartz has been used to power watches since the late 1960s. Because quartz has such a reliable and regular vibration pattern, watchmakers can channel the battery through it. This creates an extremely steady beat that helps the watch to keep time. As we can see from this example, quartz and other crystals create a very real physical energy field, and if this energy can be used to regulate mechanical devices, it can certainly be used to regulate people's energies. This is the real science behind the spiritual vibration changes that many people report when they use crystals in their healing practices. So, next time someone tells you crystals are all mumbo jumbo, you can ask them what's powering their watch!

Chi

Many assert that the idea of crystal energy has roots in the Chinese concept of life energy, or Chi. Chi is essentially the core energy of your body, your true self, or your deepest alignment. All the aspects of your mind and body flow back into your Chi energy. The things you eat, how you move your body, the people you interact with, and the practices you choose to engage in all feed into your overall Chi. So, if you are not living a happy or healthy life, your Chi will reflect this. To take proper care of your Chi, you must first take proper care of yourself. In return, your Chi creates your overall identity and helps to center your sense of self. Your Chi also connects you with the universe at large, which represents a mass or higher Chi. In a sense, the universe's Chi flows through all of us, taking individual forms but always flowing back into the same pool.

The core concept of Chi is the distinction between the formed and the formless. The formed world is the physical world, which consists of your physical body, the earth, and the people around you. These are the things we can touch, see, and feel. All of these things have a formless quality to them, even seemingly dead things like rocks, but the world of the formed only deals with the physical properties of everything. The world of the formless is the spiritual reality. It cannot be seen, heard, or perceived by the senses in any way, but it is deeply felt by everyone and everything on earth. You will not meet a person, even the staunchest atheist, who has not felt some sort of higher connection at some point in their life, whether they call it God, energy, or even just love between people. This formless world is clearly mapped onto the formed world, but the degree of their connection is paramount. These two worlds are distinct from one another, but we must find connections between them.

So, how does this relate to crystals? Well, in the world of Chi, crystals intend to form a strong connection between the formed and formless worlds. When you use crystals, you are helping to reconnect with your inner Chi energy and draw a clear connection between the formed world of your body and the formless world of your spiritual mind. When these things are in alignment, you will be in a much happier and healthier state. With crystal healing, you can create this connection, centralizing all your energies and drawing your mind and body closer than ever.

Chapter 3:
Crystals and Chakras

A nother aspect of the energy of crystals is chakras. We discussed chakras briefly when we mentioned the different energies in different parts of your body. Chakras are essentially a framework by which we can categorize our bodies according to energies. It is similar to the ideas in Chi but breaks down the energies into distinctive parts. Chakras are just as responsible for modern thought around crystal healing and form a major aspect of current crystal practice. In this chapter, I will lead you through the main concepts surrounding chakras and how you can use them to enhance your crystal practice.

What Are the Seven Chakras?

As we have mentioned, unlike Chi, there are actually multiple chakras in your body; in fact, there are seven, all responsible for a different type of energy within your body. This system identifies different key points throughout your body that can be targeted for a healing practice. When you use the chakras to heal yourself, you will be targeting one of these key areas. Each area corresponds to a different aspect of your life or potential ailment. By identifying these different areas and the part of the body with which they connect, you can construct a much more targeted spiritual healing process. In this section, I will outline the seven chakras and explain what they are, how they relate to your life and body, and how they can be used for healing.

Root Chakra

The first chakra we will be looking at is your root chakra, which is located at the lowest point in your body's core: the base of the spine. This is considered the root of your body because the entire nervous system derives from the spine. It is also the part we sit on, making it our connection to the ground below us, or our roots. This chakra connects us to the earth, forming our bonds with the ground beneath our feet and keeping us centered in reality. The root chakra is associated with the color red, indicating the blood and life force that are so central to this chakra's theme.

As with most spiritual ideas, such as astrological signs and tarot cards, all chakras have good and bad manifestations. Rather, there is a condition where this chakra is not aligned and a condition where it is. When your root chakra is misaligned, this translates to your sense of security and groundedness. Physical symptoms of a misaligned root chakra can be constipation, arthritis, or colon issues. Emotional symptoms can be anxiety about your financial or living situation and a general feeling of being lost and not knowing your place in the world. When your root chakra is aligned, you should be feeling a strong sense of control over your life and a connectedness to the world around you. Opening up this chakra and keeping it aligned is essential to maintaining your sense of self and identity from which all the other aspects of your personality will spring.

Sacral Chakra

The sacral chakra is located in the groins. This chakra governs the realms of sexuality, creativity, and self-esteem. These might seem like dissonant ideas, but they are actually closely related. For many people, the energy associated with their libido is strongly connected to their creative energy. The desire to create things, impact others, and connect are all things that apply to both creative pursuits and sexuality. Likewise, self-esteem is also related to both of these realms. Creative expression and sexuality are both very intimate topics where people show a side of themselves that they don't typically display for the whole world. You are showing a lot of vulnerability in these pursuits, and thus rejection can hurt all the more. For this reason, many people's self-esteem is firmly connected to their creative talents and sexual performance. You really can't understate the power these things have. The sacral chakra's color is orange, representing the intensity of its subject matter.

When your sacral chakra is misaligned, this can lead to issues with the associated organs. Physical symptoms might include chronic urinary tract infections, lower back pain, and sexual impotence. Emotional symptoms might include sexual repression, anxiety, or creative blocks. When your sacral chakra is blocked, you will find that these areas of your life feel like something is stuck, unable to get out. This can be a very frustrating chakra to have blocked since it governs over areas that you might feel shame around. For this reason, it can be hard to get help when this chakra is out of alignment. When your sacral chakra is aligned, though, you will experience a free flow of creative and sexual ideas. You will be able to perform well in both of these areas and feel a strong sense of self-esteem as a result. Keeping this chakra aligned is central to your sense of confidence in yourself and your abilities.

Solar Plexus Chakra

Moving upward on the body, you come to the solar plexus chakra. This chakra is located in the stomach or upper abdomen. As such, it rules things like hunger and basic needs as well as confidence and self-esteem. While the sacral chakra deals with self-esteem as related to more intimate settings, the solar plexus chakra deals with self-esteem as related to more public settings. So, while your sacral chakra might deal with your insecurities in close relationships or in the bedroom, the solar plexus chakra deals with insecurities around your body image, larger friendship groups, and things like public speaking. You'll notice a trend that the higher we move up the body, the more outward we begin to look. The first few chakras are in relation to the self, but as we approach the halfway point—the heart chakra—we begin to look more outward. The solar plexus chakra's color is yellow, and it deals with more social insecurities than the sacral chakra.

When the solar plexus chakra is misaligned or blocked, then the areas of life described above will become challenging. Physical symptoms will usually take the form of digestive issues, such as ulcers or heartburn. You might also have a lot of sensitivity to certain foods, with your stomach not being able to handle very much. In terms of psychological symptoms, you will likely suffer from a lot of confidence issues around how you are perceived. Body image issues leading to eating disorders are a common manifestation of a misaligned solar plexus chakra. For those who find their solar plexus chakra to be blocked, there might also be issues around power or feeling powerless. Therefore, if this chakra is aligned, you will likely be a very confident and sociable person. Moving forward from the confidence and groundedness of the root and sacral chakras, which are inner confidence, those with a free-flowing solar plexus chakra will also feel comfortable sharing these things with the world. They will feel like they can freely express who they are and not fear judgment of their words or appearance.

Heart Chakra

As the center chakra on the list, the heart chakra occupies a very important place. This chakra is the transition from the inner world to the outer world, bridging the connection between the self and others. It's no coincidence, then, that the facets of life this chakra deals with are love and relationships. The heart chakra is located exactly where you would think: in the middle of the chest. In yoga, this chakra is very important as the body's center, with yoga instructors often returning to this position frequently throughout the practice to re-center the body. As a transitional chakra, the heart chakra takes up a very important position on this list. It represents the crossroads between many things: self and other, inside and out, upper and lower chakras, and individualism and collectivism. The heart chakra corresponds with the color green. When you focus on your heart chakra, you are essentially focusing on core connections.

As you can imagine, having your heart chakra misaligned or blocked can leave you in a state of individualized loneliness. Failing to forge a connection between self and other will result in one of two things. On one hand, you may focus entirely too much on your own needs, never considering the needs of others. This will turn you into a highly selfish and individualistic person who no one will receive much love and care from. On the other hand, having your heart chakra misaligned could also cause you to lean in the other direction and become too focused on others' needs, completely forgoing your own. Either way, it will cause you to have very one-sided relationships that don't result in mutually beneficial and satisfactory circumstances. The misalignment of the heart chakra can also have physical symptoms, including actual heart problems and breathing problems such as asthma. Regardless of your symptoms, a blocked heart chakra will leave you in a state of deep loneliness. When your heart chakra is open, however, you will enjoy strong and fruitful connections with others in which everyone's needs are being met and everyone is able to express themselves freely.

Throat Chakra

Even higher on the body is the throat chakra, which is obviously located in the throat area. It governs parts of the body such as the mouth, tonsils, and anything in that general area. The throat chakra deals primarily with your verbal communication with others and the world. As we move up the body, we are moving further outward. While the heart chakra deals with love and connection, the throat chakra deals with all forms of communication, not necessarily of an intimate nature. The throat chakra is blue in color, and its alignment will cover a lot of your public identity, presiding over your ability to express yourself clearly to others as well as how to use your power of speech for good.

When your throat chakra is blocked, you will have problems with communication. Some physical symptoms can be throat infections or even dental problems, anything to do with the hygiene of the mouth and throat area. Emotional symptoms include a failure to express yourself properly, perhaps becoming extremely shy or simply being inarticulate. In the worst cases, those with a blocked throat chakra might start using their speech maliciously, engaging in harmful gossip or insulting behavior. You might also find that you don't have control over your speech and tend to speak without thinking. When you align this chakra properly, however, you will recapture this aspect of your speech and be able to communicate more effectively and honestly. A big part of an unblocked throat chakra is the ability to speak with compassion and remain truthful to yourself as well as to educate others.

Third Eye Chakra

Your third eye chakra is located just at your brow, a little higher than the space between your eyes. If you want, you can imagine another eye there, but that's not quite what the third eye chakra is trying to express. The third eye chakra is not about being able to see the world around you but instead being able to see past it into the intuitive world beyond. This might sound like we are going back to the base, interior world of the root chakra, but it is actually beyond even that. The third eye chakra is moving past the social world into the world of the unknown or the unformed. Your ability to trust the implicit forces around you and to see reality for what it really is are all connected to your third eye chakra. This chakra is all about reaching beyond the everyday and becoming more in touch with the vibrations of the universe. Your third eye chakra is purple. If you learn to really see through your third eye chakra, then you will have a much clearer, more intuitive picture of what is going on around you.

Those with blocked third eye chakras will often be somewhat obtuse. They are the kind of people who really can't see past the end of their noses and constantly fail to consider the bigger picture in any situation. They will not trust their intuition or even really be aware of it. Instead, they will make decisions purely based on immediate results or from information that is readily available. There are also physical symptoms associated with a third eye chakra block. Seeing and hearing problems can occur as well as chronic headaches or migraines. People who are able to open up their third eye chakra will really see the world for what it is and be able to make more long-term, spiritually aligned decisions.

Crown Chakra

The crown chakra is the top of the body's equivalent of the root chakra. This is the top of the head, or the highest extent of the nervous system. While the root chakra represents the base of all your other chakras, leading up into each of them, the crown chakra represents the apex of all your other chakras and trickles down to the others. In itself, it represents your connection to your destiny and spiritual identity. Your crown chakra should lead you through your life's path and help to align all your other chakras. They work symbiotically, each affecting the other in turn. Thus, if you don't have all your other chakras aligned, your crown chakra is likely to suffer, just as your life plans and spiritual faith tend to suffer when you are experiencing difficulty in one or another aspect of your life. Similarly, if you don't have your crown chakra fully aligned, you will likely struggle with some of your other chakras. Basically, the crown chakra cannot be properly aligned without the other chakras, and vice versa. The crown chakra corresponds either with the color indigo, to represent the apex of the color wheel, or white to represent all colors combined.

Blocked crown chakras might manifest in a number of different ways. Usually, someone with a misaligned crown chakra will seem to be a very backward or stubborn person. They will not have a strong sense of where they are going in life and will likely experience frequent ruts due to their inability to connect with their life's purpose. Often, these people will end up very lost, wasting a lot of their potential because of their inability to truly evaluate who they are or where they are going in life. They might have a strong foundation, but if they don't put it to good use, they will squander a lot of their potential. Physical symptoms might include chronic full-body pain or confusion as the entire nervous system will be affected. When you open up your crown chakra, you will find that you have set yourself on a clear course and feel strongly connected to the spiritual world above.

How to Use Crystals for Chakras

So, what does this all have to do with crystals? Well, many crystal healing practices will map themselves onto the chakra system in order to better isolate the areas of your body that need healing. Throughout the last section, I pointed out the dichotomies between a blocked and an unblocked chakra. Well, you might be wondering now how to align these misaligned or blocked chakras. This is where crystals come in. Crystals have been used throughout the centuries to create stronger connections among chakras and to help unblock the places where there have been blocks. Traditionally, crystal healers will assign different crystals to certain chakras, helping the patient to target specific crystal energies toward corresponding energies in their bodies. Certain crystals have particular powers that are more useful for some chakras than others. Sometimes, this process simply means incorporating certain crystals into your practice to target your chakras that are misaligned. Other times, this means actively touching those crystals to the part of your body corresponding to that chakra. For example, you might wear a crystal necklace if you are trying to target your throat chakra or participate in a crystal chakra healing session where crystals will be placed at different intervals along your back to match up with the chakra hierarchy. Using these methods, chakra crystal healers combine the spiritual knowledge of both crystals and chakras to help unblock and set free all aspects of your mind and body.

Chapter 4:
Crystals and Auras

The third facet of crystal healing is auras. Besides Chi, your inner core energy, and chakras, your seven central energies, you also have an external aura of energy vibrating around your body at all times. These fields are in constant motion around the perimeter of your body, modifying and influencing your every move. The concept of auras is not new. In fact, it dates back to the Ancient Greeks, using the same Greek root as the word "breeze." Thus, we can see how, from the beginning, auras were something of the air, constantly flowing and changing shape. In this chapter, we will look at the essential qualities of auras and how they can interact with the concept of crystal healing.

Aura Colors

Much like chakras all have a corresponding color, auras are usually understood through the lens of color as well. People who read auras will usually assign a specific color to someone's aura, reading the energy. This is not by accident. Colors are actually frequencies that change based on the speed at which they vibrate. On the color scale, violet has the highest frequency, while red has the lowest frequency, with the gradient of the rainbow bridging the two. If you think back to the chakras, you can see how this maps neatly onto them, with the root chakra corresponding to red, both the lowest on their respective scales, and the crown chakra corresponding to indigo, both the highest. When you read someone's color aura, you are picking up on their levels of vibration, assigning them an energy level. Colors are not just vibrations, though. Besides the chakra assignments, most people have strong associations with certain colors. Colors hold a lot of meaning, even for people who don't know about chakras at all. Once you start to learn the colors and their meanings, you will have a much easier time identifying certain color associations in your life.

How to Read Auras

Auras take a special kind of person to read. You need to have both a keen eye and a strong sense of the person and who they are. If you are going to read an aura, make sure you spend some time with the person first. When someone knows you better, they will be able to let their guard down and allow their full personality to shine through. Once they are in this state, you must concentrate very closely on the line between them and the wall. This is where the aura lies. If you look very closely, you should be able to see the faint outline of a certain color radiating just around the edge of their body. You can also read your own aura. To do this, you will need to hold up your hand in front of a wall or stand in front of a mirror. From there, you should be able to discern your aura. Once you have determined your or another person's aura, you will be able to interpret it.

What Do Auras Mean?

So, you've figured out your aura color, now what does it mean? Well, there are several ways to interpret the colors of your aura. One is to map your aura color onto its corresponding chakra. If your aura is associated with a chakra, it generally means that that chakra is unblocked for you. Furthermore, it might even mean that you are particularly ruled by that chakra, with your basic personality aligning closely with that chakra's qualities. You can think of this as being similar to your astrological sign, with a particular facet of life that you are focused on. So, if your aura is red, you are likely a very grounded person who is probably a rock for others in your life with a strong sense of self and purpose. If your aura is orange, you might be a particularly sexual person who has a strong penchant for passion and connection. People with yellow auras are usually the life of the party with a wide social circle. People with a green aura will likely have very close intimate relationships in their life and be exceptionally caring. If your aura is blue, it might mean that you are a very verbal person who communicates remarkably well and takes a lot of pride in your language skills. If you possess a purple aura, you are most likely a very spiritual person with strong foresight. And finally, if your aura is indigo, then you are most definitely a powerfully aligned person who finds balance in most facets of your life. Through all these colors, we can see how colored auras can have a powerful impact on how you conduct yourself throughout your life and what forms your base personality.

How Crystals Affect Auras

So, how can crystals interact with your aura? Similar to how certain crystals have corresponding chakras, they also have corresponding auras. You can choose a specific crystal to heal the specific aura that it has a relationship with. But, you might ask, if auras are just something that describes your personality and values, much like an astrological sign, then what needs healing? We know that chakras can become misaligned, so what can happen to auras? Well, auras have their own version of misalignment, which is called an auric tear. Auric tears are vulnerable points within your aura that risk letting negative energy into your body. If you are experiencing an auric tear, then you might have anxiety, depression, or general misalignment. Things just might seem to never go your way. Enter crystals. When you are experiencing difficulties with the areas of your life that correspond to your aura, you need to do something about it. You can use the vibrations of various crystals to help restore your aura back to the state it is meant to be in. When you do so, you are creating a protective layer around your aura, which works to heal existing auric tears and prevent future ones. As always, crystals are there to help align and center your energies.

Pillar 2:
Sources

Moving on to the second pillar of crystals, we arrive at sources. When you are planning to use crystals in your healing practice, you will need to know how to get them. Not all crystal sources are made equal, so you will have to do a little bit of research to ensure that you are buying the right product and not engaging with fake or inferior crystals. In this pillar, we will dive into everything you need to know about sourcing, helping you to figure out the best place to purchase your crystals.

Chapter 5:
What to Buy

The first step in obtaining your crystals is figuring out which ones you want to buy. The world of crystals is so vast and complex that it can really be hard to know where to start. You might have a wide range of interests in their healing power as well as ailments you want to fix, so choosing just one or a few crystals can be extremely difficult. For this reason, you need to seek out all the information you can possibly find on crystals and crystal healing in order to determine the precise crystals you need. In terms of crystals, there are a few primary factors to consider when determining what kind of crystals you should buy. In this chapter, I will give you some concrete guidance on how to identify and choose crystals.

Crystal Shapes

Back in Chapter 1, I stated that crystals are defined by their molecular structure. Well, there are actually several different molecular structures that crystals can take on, each denoting a different quality. Understanding the meanings of these different molecular structures can help you to better identify what kinds of crystals you want to buy. There are seven main shapes in the world of crystals, all of which convey their own unique meaning.

1. Cube Crystals

Crystals that come in cube shapes are grounding crystals. Much like the root chakra, these crystals help keep you grounded and remind you of the simpler, basic things in life that are important to keep in mind.

2. Pyramid Crystals

When you buy crystals in the shape of a pyramid, you are intending to connect with your desires. This shape resonates with the sacral chakra, which deals with passion and pleasure. Manifesting with pyramid crystals will help you connect with the things you really want.

3. Sphere Crystals

Sphere crystals resemble a planet or a globe, resonating with their purpose of connecting you with the greater world as a whole. These crystals can help put your life into perspective, reminding you of the greater forces at work in the universe.

4. Tumbled Crystals

These are the smallest form of crystal and come in tiny shapes much like a pebble. These are travel-sized crystals that can help you continue to feel a crystal's energy everywhere you go. You can also make these into jewelry so you always have a crystal touching your skin for protection.

5. Pointed Crystals

These crystals focus on… well, focus! If you have a very specific goal or problem to target, then manifesting with pointed crystals is an excellent idea. You will be able to sharply focus on your task at hand, channeling energy in a very specific way.

6. Heart Crystals

While crystals don't naturally occur in heart shapes, they can be cut as such to enhance their overall meaning. Using a heart-shaped crystal is intended to channel your heart chakra, helping you to connect with others and show your compassion.

7. Cluster Crystals

Using a cluster crystal is all about unity and connection. Much like the crown chakra, the cluster crystal presides over all the other crystals, helping them to bind together and form a cohesive healing pattern.

Choosing a Crystal

The next step comes when you have to decide what actual crystal type you want to choose. In Chapter 17, I will list a more definitive selection of crystals, but here I'll outline some important factors for you to consider when choosing a crystal to purchase. First of all, you should be very clear about your intentions with your crystals. If you don't state up front what you want out of your crystal journey, then you will be more lost than you need to be. Being aware right away of what you want your crystals to do for you will help you in the initial narrowing process. The second step in choosing a crystal is discovering things about yourself. We've already talked about crystals and auras to help you to choose a crystal that particularly corresponds to your aura, but you might also want to consider your astrological sign in the mix. As I stated in the crystal history section, European crystal practice traditionally associated people's astrological signs with crystals. Take a look at your birth chart and make a list of crystals that correspond to some of your major signs, specifically your sun, moon, and rising signs. From there, you will have a definitive list of your intentions with your crystals and the ones that will particularly help you in your own personal journey. And finally, once you have made these lists, you can simply choose the crystals you gravitate toward. Colors or shapes that draw you in might be your subconscious looking for those crystal properties in your life. As with most spiritual practices, intuition lies at the core of your crystal healing practice.

Chapter 6:
Where to Buy

O nce you have decided on which crystals or what kinds of crystals you want to buy, then you will have to start looking for sources. This can be just as confusing a task as choosing crystals in the first place. With the recent boom in crystal popularity, it seems like crystal stores are popping up all over the place, both online and in physical locations. For a person who wants to start getting into crystals, the options can seem overwhelming. You might find that there is just too much out there for you to feel like you can make an informed decision. Luckily, in this chapter, I will provide you with some guidance on the main sources people use to get their crystals as well as a helpful guide for identifying which crystals are authentic and which aren't. By the end of the chapter, you should have a firm sense of where you want to buy your crystals.

Buying in Person

The first thing that sprang to mind for you when thinking about buying crystals was likely going into a store. You probably imagined a long row full of boxes containing sparkly stones, each brimming with hidden power. However, there are actually a lot of different contexts in which you can buy crystals in person. In this section, we will look at the different aspects of buying crystals in person as well as the pros and cons of doing so.

Types of In-Person Crystal Sources

As you can imagine, there are many ways to buy your crystals in person. You may have even encountered some of these sources in your life. Here, we will look at some of the most common types of crystal retailers and their qualities.

Occult Stores

Often, crystals are sold alongside other occult or spirituality wares in a general-purpose occult store. These places are good because they offer a wide variety of other spiritual items and are generally more common than crystal-only stores. However, you might find that, depending on the size of the store, there will be a more limited crystal selection and the staff might be less knowledgeable about crystal healing.

Crystal Stores

Sometimes, you will come across a store that sells only crystals. These are far less common and will generally only be found in major towns and cities. They are, however, one of the better options since they tend to have an excellent selection of different types and cuts of crystals as well as a very knowledgeable staff.

Independent or Market Salespeople

Occasionally, independent sellers will set up temporary stalls in market-places or run a crystal business alongside their psychic or tarot reading practice. These people can be more hit-or-miss than more permanent crystal and occult stores. On one hand, you might get someone who is extremely knowledgeable and passionate and who can use some other psychic skills they have to personally tailor crystals to your life situation. However, there is also more room for dishonesty here, meaning you run more risk of being sold fake crystals, being overcharged, or possibly even being scammed. If you are going with an independent seller, make sure they are trustworthy.

Pros and Cons of Buying in Person

Obviously, there are some benefits as well as drawbacks to buying crystals in person. As you go through your crystal journey, you will gradually figure out what you prefer. Here, we will explore some of the pros and cons of in-person crystal shopping.

Pros of Buying in Person

The most obvious upside of buying in person is that you get to have a physical experience with your crystals before purchasing them. Provided the owner lets you, browsing a crystal store will involve physically holding the crystals you are intending to buy. From this, you can get a clearer sense of that crystal's vibrations. The intuitive aspect of crystal shopping that I mentioned at the end of Chapter 5 will be much easier to lean into at an in-person store. You might find that you are drawn to a crystal you didn't expect to be all because you were able to see and touch it in person first. You will also be able to interact more with the owner or staff and, provided they are knowledgeable, discuss your crystal intentions with them. All in all, in-person shopping gives you a more personalized, intimate experience with your crystals before you buy them.

Cons of Buying in Person

The main downside of buying your crystals in person is availability and selection. Not everyone lives in a big city that has a lot of crystal store options to choose from. You might be stuck with a very small store that has incredibly limited options. When it comes to market stalls and independent sellers, you might run into the problem of lack of accountability. You might buy a crystal from a retailer that turns out to be fake, but if they have up and gone, you have no one to give you a refund. Always make sure to keep the business card or contact information of anyone you buy from. All in all, though, if you are willing to travel to a bigger crystal store, you should do at least some of your crystal shopping in person, just for the physical connection.

Buying Online

If you live in a more remote location or find traveling difficult, you might want to look toward buying crystals online. A large portion of the recent surge in crystal popularity has happened online, so you will find that there is a huge variety of options for buying your crystals through an online space. Likely, you have already encountered some crystal people on social media who may have associated stores, so you are no stranger to the online crystal business. In this section, I will give you some important guidance on how to buy crystals online.

Types of Online Crystal Sources

As with in-person stores, there are a lot of different ways you can buy crystals online. Many different kinds of people and companies sell crystals online, from the most independent crystal healers to large corporations like Amazon. You will certainly find no shortage of crystals online, which is why it can be somewhat overwhelming to choose where you should be looking for them. Here, we will give you an overview of the three most common types of online crystal stores to help you decide where you want to seek out your crystal collection.

Mega-Retailers

Since crystals have taken off so much recently, many larger retailers have begun selling them. You will certainly find a large variety of crystals on certain mass retailer websites, such as Amazon, Aliexpress, and Shien. These larger corporations might lack personal connection, but they make up for it in price. You will usually find the lowest prices for crystals on these websites, so if you are a crystal user on a budget, then this might be where you want to turn. However, for those who are very new to crystals, these websites don't offer very much guidance, so you might find yourself overwhelmed. Mega-retailers are ideal for those who already know exactly what they want and are searching for the lowest possible price.

Online Crystal Stores

A step down in size from the mega-retailers are online stores dedicated to selling crystals. These are usually run by crystal healers or enthusiasts and thus will be able to offer much more guidance about what kinds of crystals you should buy. Some might even be accompanied by blogs that explain the complex meanings behind each crystal. Many online crystal stores are still large enough to have a wide selection and, in fact, might even have a wider selection than the crowd-pleasing mega-retailers who only stock the most popular crystals. Thus, if you are looking for more obscure crystals or a little more guidance around the crystals you want to buy, then you should look toward specialized online crystal stores.

Spirituality Influencers

The most independent sellers you will find online—the virtual equivalent of the marketplace stall—are social media crystal influencers. Many of these people run blogs, Instagram pages, or TikTok accounts dedicated to crystals. If you learned something about crystals from these people, you might be incentivized to buy from them. Many of these influencers offer a highly personalized crystal experience. Depending on how popular and busy they are, they might even be available to personally chat with you to discuss your crystal needs. Some will sell through their own personal website and some through larger platforms like Etsy. However, be aware of the same dangers as with independent in-person retailers and be sure to get their correct contact information before buying from an independent online retailer to avoid any scams. If something seems fishy, it's best to avoid it.

Pros and Cons of Buying Online

As you can see, there are a lot of reasons to buy your crystals online, but there are still things you have to be aware of and watch out for. Here, we will look at the positive and negative aspects of online crystal shopping.

Pros of Buying Online

What online shopping really has going for it is availability. You are no longer limited by the options at your local crystal shop or required to drive to faraway cities to find the crystals you want. If you're looking for something more obscure, you can bet that you will be able to find it online sooner than in person. Online shopping also might cut out the middleman. You don't always know where in-person crystal retailers source their crystals, especially the more independent ones. For all you know, it might be an online store! Buying online is also often cheaper for this very reason since the retailers don't have to pay rent on a store-front or staff to work there. So, for those who want to save a bit of money and time, as well as access a much wider array of crystal options, online is likely the best option.

Cons of Buying Online

Online shopping's biggest flaw has always been a lack of certainty about the product before you buy. This is usually a big problem for things like clothes, which aren't guaranteed to fit, and it can be just as big a problem for crystals. Holding a crystal in your hand is the only sure way to know if you connect with it. Even if you do all the research you can, shopping online will always lack this physical aspect. You might also miss out on some personalized help. Barring certain crystal influencers, there really isn't much personalized help online. If you are more of a beginner who is looking to talk to someone about your crystal needs, then you will certainly be lacking for this online. All in all, the online option is recommended more for intermediate to advanced crystal practitioners, with beginners requiring more guidance than many online platforms are able to provide.

Identifying Crystal Authenticity

As I stated a few times above, there are a lot of opportunities for people to sell you fake or subpar crystals. Especially if you are a beginner in your crystal journey, you might have a difficult time discerning what's real from what's fake. And since you are intent on harnessing the very real power of authentic crystals, you don't want to get stuck with something fake. Fake crystals that don't have the same chemical qualities as real crystals simply won't work. If you attempt to heal using fake crystals, you will not get results and may become discouraged with the crystal healing practice altogether. Here, we will discuss some of the aspects of crystal fakery and what you can do to protect yourself from it.

What Is a Fake Crystal?

So, what is the difference between a real crystal and a fake one? Well, it's all in the chemical composition. You see, real crystals always come from the earth. They are naturally formed substances that absorb earthly vibrations and energy. However, some sellers will provide crystals that are not naturally formed in the earth but are instead man-made. This could be a manipulated rock that is dyed or shaped to look like a crystal or a completely artificial substance like fiberglass that is artificially shaped to resemble a crystal. These things are simply not crystals and will not work in the same way. Trying to pass them off as authentic crystals is wrong and does a lot of harm to the crystal community. Unfortunately, these things still circulate, so you have to be wary of them.

Red Flags for Fake Crystals

Fortunately, there are some clear "tells" when a crystal is not authentic. Most crystal healers will have a keen eye for what a crystal should look like, but for a beginner, it can be really difficult. In this section, I will describe some clear red flags around crystal shopping to help you identify crystals that might not be real.

Red Flag #1: Shady Selling Practices

Right off the bat, you should be evaluating the perceived honesty of the seller. Dishonesty can happen at any level, from a street vendor to a major chain retailer. For this reason, you can't always judge by appearances, but you should judge by the way the product is being sold. Are there clear indications of what the crystal is made of? Does it seem to be factory-made or mass-produced? Is it being pushed on you with very vague information or a lot of haste? All of these things can indicate a shady crystal business that is not selling the real thing. Whether you are buying online or in person, you need to keep a sharp eye out for these "snake oil" salespeople.

Red Flag #2: Strange Names

One of the most common ways to spot a fake crystal is if it has a weird or fake-sounding name. All crystals have official geological names like amethyst, quartz, jade, and so on. Normally, when you are buying crystals, they will simply be called these names. However, for some reason, many fake crystal sellers will add descriptors to these existing geological names, calling them "sunset quartz" or "starry night amethyst." These are often actually dyed quartz (which is not a real gem) or even just glass. Reputable crystal salespeople will not need to use these quirky or mystical-sounding names because they trust their product and their customers enough to be up front and authentic. Even though they might sound cool, these funky-named crystals are often fake.

Red Flag #3: Too Perfect-Looking

Real crystals come from the ground and thus have irregular coloring and shapes. When you look at real marble flooring, you can see how the lines in the marble are naturally formed. The same goes for real wood, which will have organic-looking lines throughout. Well, crystals will also have these same kinds of patterns. Fake crystals, on the other hand, often will have more regular patterns, since they are man-made and not formed in the earth. Even though the manufacturer might try to make the formation look natural, most people will be able to see through this pretty quickly. Look closely at the formation of the crystal and judge for yourself whether it looks like it could be a rock that came from the ground. If it doesn't look like it, then you might be dealing with a fake crystal.

Chapter 7:
Vogel Crystals

In the world of crystals, there is one innovator in particular who stands above the rest. His name was Marcel Vogel, and he was one of the pioneering crystal scientists of the 20th century. Vogel worked for IBM developing scientific principles behind things like crystal-powered computers and watches. He also authored some of the most important writings on crystals and how to utilize their power properly. One of the most influential things he came up with was a particular way to cut crystals that harnesses their power in the most efficient way possible. These crystals, cut according to Vogel's research, are called Vogel crystals and are considered one of the highest-quality crystal cuts in the world. In this chapter, we will explore different aspects of the Vogel crystal, exploring what makes it one of the best ways to cut crystals and how you can find and identify a Vogel crystal for yourself!

How Do Vogel Crystals Work?

First of all, all Vogel crystals are quartz. You won't really find a Vogel crystal in any other material. This is because quartz is one of the purest crystals and thus has the ability to channel more effectively than others. In terms of shape, the Vogel crystal is cut in a very specific way with one point at both ends. The idea is that one end acts as a receiving port and the other as a transmission antenna. You can think of these like the speaker and microphone on a headset, with one end for input and one for output. The idea is that this cut harnesses the natural vibrations of the crystal in the best way possible and thus has the ability to transmit energy at a much more efficient rate. This cut is also used for technological purposes as it is able to channel the quartz's vibrations very efficiently into the battery of a computer or watch. You can still get effective results with non-Vogel quartz, of course, but this is considered the height of crystal innovation. For these reasons, many crystal practitioners opt for Vogel crystals to ensure they are practicing crystal healing to its fullest potential.

How to Identify a Vogel Crystal

Considering these qualities of the Vogel crystal, you are probably curious about how to identify whether a crystal is a Vogel crystal. Here, I will provide you with the basic criteria for something to be considered a Vogel crystal.

1. **Natural Quartz**

   For a crystal to be considered Vogel, it has to be a naturally occurring crystal. You cannot make a Vogel crystal without completely natural quartz because the vibrations simply will not work.

2. Doubly Terminated

Double termination is the technical name for the Vogel crystal shape, which comes to a point at either end. Furthermore, the crystal must be shaped to this arrangement with the exact right measurements as specified by the Vogel design. You should make sure it comes from a certified cutter so you know you are getting the exact right shape.

3. Cut With the C-Axis

All quartz has a "c-axis" which is the natural molecular structure of the crystal. You can think of this as being like the grain of wood. You want your crystals to be cut with the grain rather than against it so that they are as smooth as possible and able to conduct energy with maximum efficiency. Vogel crystals are stipulated to be cut along this axis.

4. 51-Degree Reception End

The reception end of the crystal, sometimes known as the female end, must be cut at an angle of 51 degrees. This is a reference to the dimensions of the Great Pyramid of Giza, which inundates the crystal with more power. Connecting with one of the most important monuments of the ancient world helps to center the spiritual energy of the crystal.

5. Less Than 51 Degree Transmitter End

Your transmitter end, sometimes known as the male end, must have a more acute angle than the reception end. The idea behind this is to refine the energy as it passes through the crystal. If you have a wider receiver than transmitter, the crystal is working to focus the energy flowing through itself, thus creating a more accurate channel.

6. Four or More Side Faces

Another essential attribute of a Vogel crystal is the number of sides it has. Your crystal must have at least four sides in order to be considered a bona fide Vogel crystal.

How Can I Use Vogel Crystals

Vogel crystals are very useful for focusing energy. Many people approach crystal practice with a very unfocused mind. They are searching for meaning and purpose in their lives and thus want to find some kind of focus for their thoughts and goals. Incorporating a Vogel crystal into your practice is an excellent way to add some of that extra razor-sharp focus to your life. One great way to use Vogel crystals is to approach them with a question that you are agonizing over or a problem that feels like it is running in circles through your mind. The Vogel crystal will help you gain clarity on these messy situations and give you guidance as to the direction you should be going in life.

Pillar 3:
Purposes

As you can probably see from all the previous chapters, there are a lot of ways you can use crystals. Crystal healing is obviously the most common, which we will get into in Pillar 4, but there are also many other ways that you can implement crystals in your life. They are all important to consider and give you an opportunity to integrate crystals deeper into your life and practices. These other uses will help you practice crystal healing more casually and frequently. They allow you to make crystals a part of your everyday life, not just your dedicated practice. In this pillar, we will look at three distinctive ways in which you can use crystals. The first way is around your house by decorating with crystals. The second way is to wear crystals on your body so that their powers can always be with you. And the third way is to incorporate crystals into your existing meditation practices. With these three methods, you can see that there are more integrated and diverse ways to use your crystals.

Chapter 8:
Decoration

Who doesn't love the idea of beautiful crystals all over your house? Incorporating crystals into your home's decor is one of the most interesting ways to bring energy flow into your everyday life. Having crystals around the house can help you to recalibrate your energies throughout the day without even having to engage in active crystal practice. They can bring a sense of peace and balance to your spaces, inundating your home with their healing powers. As a nice bonus, they also lend a great aesthetic as decorations! Many crystal practitioners incorporate crystals into their home decor for these reasons.

One of the most important things to consider when decorating with crystals is the compatibility of the crystal's qualities and the uses for the specific space. Each room in your house has a particular purpose and thus a particular energy profile you want to follow. Failing to consider the specific uses for the rooms you are intending to decorate with crystals is one of the biggest mistakes you can make. Let's just say you don't want to put high-energy crystals in the bedroom or relaxation crystals in your home office. When you are decorating your house with crystals, the ways in which each room is used are of the utmost importance. In this chapter, I will lead you through a room-by-room guide for what kinds of crystals work best in certain spaces.

Exteriors

The first part of this chapter will not be devoted to your house but to the space around your house. It might not seem like it, but your outdoor spaces provide lots of opportunities to incorporate crystals. Since outdoor spaces look different for every house, you should really consider what yours looks like and how you use it. Whether you have a small balcony or a sprawling yard, there are many different ways to spend time outside. Maybe you have a dedicated eating area where you love to entertain and have dinner parties, or perhaps you have a cozy hammock area surrounded by tranquil ferns where you love to go and read. You might even have a large enough space to play sports or do your morning exercises. Deciding what kind of energy you want to be encouraging all depends on your specific uses for your outdoor space. In this section, I will walk you through some of the considerations around outdoor crystal design.

Types of Crystals to Use

As I said above, the types of crystals you will choose for your outdoor space will hinge significantly on what kind of outdoor space you have. For eating and entertaining outdoor areas, you want to use crystals that enhance connection and pleasure. Eating with others is one of the most powerful ways to connect, so what better way to streamline that connection energy than with a crystal? If you use your outdoor area for relaxation purposes, then you want to choose crystals that focus on meditation and rejuvenation. Relaxation is all about recharging your batteries, so cleansing and tranquilizing crystals are perfect for a relaxation area. Finally, if you are using your outdoor area for sports or exercise, especially practices like yoga, then you want to choose crystals that forge a mind-body connection and ground you in the earth. We go outside to exercise because it better connects us to the earth around us, so crystals that focus on spiritual connection are great for this purpose. Putting some serious thought into the purpose of your outdoor space will help you choose the crystals you want to incorporate there.

How to Incorporate Them

Backyard decorations can be as creative as you want them to be, so why not integrate some crystals? One creative way to add crystals to your outdoor space is by making them into a beautiful set of chimes. You can make one from scratch or add your favorite crystals to an existing chime. You can also use crystals in tiling, creating a tile display at the center of your outdoor table or to attach to a tree. The most important thing about crystal incorporation is to place them strategically. If you want to enhance connections while eating, then you should place your crystals at the center of the table to help channel the energy toward one cohesive center. Likewise, you should include your crystals in the specific area of your outdoor space that you use the most. However you choose to incorporate your crystals into your space, make sure it's creative and cohesive!

Bedroom

Moving indoors, many people decorate with crystals in their bedrooms. The bedroom is actually a more multipurpose room than you might think. People obviously use their bedrooms for sleeping, but they are also used for dressing, grooming, and intimate relations. Some people even work at a desk set up in their bedroom or read books in bed, among many other things. That's a lot of purposes for one room! Thus, when considering the vibrations you want your bedroom to have, you have to find a way to center them all. Try to think about all the ways in which you use your bedroom and all the different energies you want to enhance there. You might find that you want to use different crystals in different parts of your bedroom to try to section off the sometimes conflicting energies there. Here, we will look at the best ways to use crystals in your bedroom.

Types of Crystals to Use

Similar to using crystals outside, you will want to use a few different types of crystals in order to focus different kinds of energies in your bedroom. The first major use for your bedroom is sleeping. You might think to just use relaxation crystals here, but there is actually so much more to sleeping than just relaxing. Sleeping and dreaming are very important processes for brain development, imagination, memory, and spiritual identity. Dreams can be very powerful experiences, either for good or bad. You likely want to use a few different kinds of crystals to enhance your sleep: one to relax and wind down from the day, one to encourage positive dreams, and one to encourage meditation or philosophical thought. Combining these will ensure that you have relaxing and fruitful sleep. The second major use for the bedroom is intimacy and sex. Whether you have multiple partners a week or have been happily married for decades, you likely want to bring some element of excitement to your bedroom. Crystals that encourage arousal, pleasure, and comfort in the body are essential here. Self-esteem is crucial for a healthy sex life, so you want to forge a strong connection with your own body in order to explore someone else's. Speaking of comfort in your body, you will also want to encourage self-esteem in relation to the third most common use for the bedroom, which is dressing and grooming. Feeling like you can put together a strong look that complements your body and makes you feel good about yourself is essential. Crystals that encourage mind-body connection and confidence are great for your dressing and grooming area. No matter the use, there is a crystal to help you in the bedroom.

How to Incorporate Them

Bedrooms are a great place to bring crystals since there are so many hidden places for you to put them. The trick with such a versatile room is to strategically place certain crystals to enhance the different uses of the bedroom. So, for crystals that are intended to help you sleep, you should place them lower down and closer to where your head is when you sleep. The bedside table or your headboard can be great places for these crystals to radiate into your mind while you sleep. During intimacy, you might be more upright on the bed, so you might want to place these aphrodisiac crystals on a higher plane, perhaps hanging on the wall above the headboard to create a second layer of psychic space. Finally, for dressing purposes, you should incorporate these crystals around your vanity. You could create a crystal frame for your mirror or have a crystal dish for your precious jewelry. By sectioning off different places to put your crystals, you are helping to compartmentalize the room and keep all the different energies separate so they don't conflict with one another.

Kitchen

One of the most dynamic rooms in the house is the kitchen. The kitchen is a place for many things. It is a place for creativity, enjoyment, pleasure, and connection. Some people describe the kitchen as the heart of the home, so you want to make sure that this room has the right energy. Crystals are a great way to enhance the flow of your kitchen, bring people together, and stimulate creativity in your culinary activities. When you use crystals in the kitchen, you are giving yourself an opportunity to push yourself toward a happier family and a better life for all. Here, we will look at some of the best ways to incorporate crystals into your kitchen.

Types of Crystals to Use

Since we mentioned that the kitchen is like the heart of the house, you would do very well to use crystals connected with the heart chakra. This will help center the room in the house and redirect flow from other rooms back to the kitchen. The heart chakra is also all about love and intimate family connections, bringing the closest people in your life together. Eating together, cooking together, and doing so in the presence of crystals can really help strengthen your connection with your family. You might also want to use some creativity-stimulating crystals, ones that help you connect with your imagination and that will motivate you to try new things in the kitchen. These two types of crystals will help you balance connection and creativity in your food-preparing spaces.

How to Incorporate Them

Where you place the crystals will depend on the type you are using. For connection-based crystals, place them where your family normally gathers to eat. This could be your eat-in kitchen space, your breakfast bar, or even your dining room table. Creating a beautiful centerpiece out of crystals can be a great way to seamlessly introduce crystals into your food spaces. For creativity-sparking crystals, you want to put these where you will be actively preparing the food. Try placing some crystals on your windowsill or hanging them above the oven or main prep space. Using these two methods, you can bring a distinct sense of strength and purpose to your kitchen space.

Living Room

The living room is also a space that is focused on connection, but a slightly different kind. While the bedroom focuses on connection with the self and intimate partner, the most intimate form of connection, and the kitchen focuses on connection with the immediate family, the living room is the space that has the strongest relationship to the outside world. This will be the space where you spend time both with your immediate family and with visitors. Thus, you want to focus on energies that are both homey and connected but also inviting and outward-reaching. You can think of this space as your home's gateway to the world beyond, creating an inviting atmosphere for everyone to enjoy. Here, we will look at the best ways to create this environment in your living room using crystals.

Types of Crystals to Use

Crystals that enhance interpersonal connections are the obvious choice for the living room. The purpose of the room is for conversation and bonding, either with family or friends, so you want to bring in crystals that bring people together. Another important aspect of the living room to harness is a sense of open-mindedness. This is the room through which new perspectives and ideas will be introduced to your home, so you should create a space that invites those new ideas in. For this reason, openness and welcoming crystals are ideal picks for your living room. Choose these wisely, and you will create energy that invites anyone in and makes them feel like a close family member.

How to Incorporate Them

The living room is typically a well-decorated room full of trinkets, so you will likely find many opportunities to incorporate them. One great place to put crystals in your living room is near the fireplace if you have one. The expression "home and hearth" emphasizes the fireplace, or hearth, as the heart of the living room. This is the component that releases heat and is the focal point of the room. Even if you are not actively lighting it, many living rooms with fireplaces arrange their furniture around it so it acts as a kind of psychic focus. Placing crystals on your mantel will thus help spread their energy around the room evenly. You can also place crystals on the coffee table, especially if this is a place where you are serving snacks. Using these centering methods, you can create a strong circulation of positive and inviting energy in your living room.

Chapter 9:
Wearing Crystals

A nother effective way to passively incorporate crystals into your life is by wearing them. Wearable crystals have a very long tradition. Many jewelry practices and styles in cultures around the world have incorporated crystals. To this day, it's extremely easy to buy crystal jewelry, even without realizing you are doing so or knowing anything about crystals. Chances are, you actually already own a piece of crystal jewelry and don't even know it! But if you are aware of the benefits and select your crystals right, there are so many ways wearing crystals can help improve your life! In this chapter, I will talk about how wearing crystals can help you as well as the things you should consider when selecting a crystal to wear around with you.

Benefits of Wearing Crystals

There are numerous benefits to crystal healing, and many of those can be especially enjoyed when you are wearing your crystals around. For this reason, many people swear by their crystal bracelets or necklaces. People also wear their crystals as earrings or even have tiny ones stuffed inside their bras! There are countless ways to benefit from your wearable crystals. Here, we will look at some of the most compelling ways wearable crystals can help you.

Integrating Your Crystal Practice

Depending on your crystal practice, you might have isolated times of day when you engage with your crystals. These might be during meditation or crystal healing sessions. Doing these things is great since it gives you some solid, dedicated crystal time. However, it is also helpful to integrate your crystal practice into your life more continuously. If you wear your crystals throughout the day, you will be able to reap their benefits all the time rather than just during isolated occasions. You might also be able to benefit even when you are not paying attention to your crystals, meaning that you are achieving a subconscious symbiosis. Essentially, wearable crystals make your crystal practice a 24/7 occasion.

Creating a More Intuitive Mind

Because of this stronger and more consistent connection to your crystals, you will likely forge a deeper connection with your subconscious. You will be letting your subconscious mind become more vocal in your relationship, allowing it to speak louder to you. After a while, you will likely find that you have an easier time listening to and learning from your intuition. From this, you can really see how constantly wearing crystals can lead to a much more intuitive mind overall, even after you have taken your crystal jewelry off.

Health Benefits

Many healers will also preach the physical health benefits of wearable crystals. Ailments such as skin conditions and arthritis can benefit a lot from prolonged contact with vibrating crystals. You might find that wearing crystals can have a positive effect on some of these ailments. Talk to your doctor or homeopathic care provider to discuss whether you might be able to incorporate crystals into your existing healing practice for these things.

Aesthetics

Let's be honest, another major attraction of crystals is how they look! With all the beautiful colors, shapes, and textures that come out of the crystal family, they make wonderful jewelry even without considering their healing powers. You can buy or make some truly beautiful jewelry from your crystal collection to wear in style while also benefiting from their powerful energies.

Things to Consider

Before you start strapping on your quartz necklaces and jade bracelets, you should give some careful consideration to what they are going to be used for. Wearing crystals and constantly absorbing their energy can actually be very draining, and if you don't consider their uses, you might end up confusing your energies around certain activities. Wearing a crystal around your body is much more drastic than incorporating it into your practice. The wearing of a crystal involves constant contact with that crystal's vibrations and thus means that you will be more closely and consistently exposed to its energy. In this section, we will explore some aspects of crystal wearing that should be considered before you start.

Context Matters

As with decorating your home, you need to cater your crystals to the situation at hand. Wearing the wrong crystal at the wrong event or to the wrong location can have serious consequences on the energy you are bringing into that situation. Think back to our discussion of the home and the energies involved in the different rooms. Now think of your life as being like a house, with different rooms that serve different purposes. Your life is full of diverse experiences that all require different energy levels and types of energy to flow properly. You're probably going to want to bring different energy levels to your workplace than you would bring when hanging out with friends or on a relaxing day at the beach. All these contexts will require you to have different energies. Bringing a relaxation-focused crystal to a work brainstorming session would likely not be a good idea, just as bringing a focus crystal to your Saturday night out on the town may not be optimal either. These can confuse your energies and make your experience worse and unfulfilling. When choosing crystals to wear for your various experiences, make sure to tailor them to the energy you want to bring into that experience.

Be Careful About Who You Interact With

Another facet of life that has a lot of variabilities is the social world. Besides where you are going, it also matters who you are with. Crystals will also affect those around you, their energies subtly radiating to the other person. Thus, you should carefully consider who you are with and how the crystals you are wearing might affect them as well as the general dynamic between you. You certainly don't want to encourage any romantic feelings between you and your boss or contentious feelings between you and your new partner's family. Making sure that you are wearing crystals that encourage the type of relationship you want to have with the person or people with whom you are interacting and that nourish their natural energy is essential to a healthy crystal-wearing practice.

Give Yourself a Break

Finally, wearing crystals constantly, especially very intense crystals, can be exhausting. Some crystals have very strong energy and encourage a lot of change and rebirth, which you don't always want to be bringing to your life every day. If you have a favorite crystal necklace that you find yourself wearing frequently and you are noticing that its vibrations are affecting you a lot, then you should consider giving yourself a break from that crystal, maybe leaving it off for a day to see how you feel or avoiding wearing it in situations that don't suit its energy. Remember: Your crystals should be serving you, not the other way around, so if you ever feel like the energy is too strong, you can always take a break.

Chapter 10:
Meditation

Meditation is one of the fastest-growing practices in the West. Over the past few decades, more and more people on this side of the world, even those who don't practice Buddhism or Hinduism, are discovering the amazing benefits of meditation. Mindfulness and meditation have even taken over in the corporate world, with many workplaces offering mindfulness workshops for their employees. In the age of hustle culture and mass burnout, with a pandemic on top of it all, it's no wonder many people are finding meditation beneficial. It can help refocus your mind and rid yourself of some of the more harmful mindsets you may get into. It can even help improve your physical health by reducing stress. Suffice it to say, there are a number of reasons meditation is becoming so popular these days. Crystals are also very popular, leading many people to incorporate them into their meditation practice. In this chapter, I will talk all about the purposes, benefits, and methods of using crystals to meditate.

Why Meditate With Crystals?

Alongside meditation in popularity are crystals, so it's no wonder that many people have been combining them. In fact, the practice of meditating with crystals dates back to the very origins of crystal practice itself, so putting the two together makes a lot of sense. Meditation is all about letting the energies of the universe pass through you as you absorb and attempt to be at one with them. So, why not incorporate some of the specific energies from crystals into that practice? Crystals can work to give your meditation more focus and help with some of the main purposes of crystals, such as manifestation and energy absorption. If there is a crystal whose energy you are particularly interested in or a particular conundrum in your life that you want to bring focus to, then incorporating crystals into your meditation practice can be a great idea. In short, meditating with crystals can enhance both your meditation practice and crystal practice, creating something that is greater than the sum of its parts. Here, we will look at some of the most compelling reasons to use crystals in your meditation practice, illustrating some of the ways they can help push you further along in your spiritual journey.

Focus

The first main reason you might use crystals in your meditation practice is to try to focus on a specific issue or question. This relates to the more Western meaning of the word "meditate," which means to ponder or think over. In Western culture, meditation is often associated with Christian monks or philosophers who would spend their days pondering theological questions, poetry, and art. With this type of meditative practice, you are trying to use the power of crystals to really think a question through. It could be a personal question, such as whether or not you should pursue a relationship with someone, a professional question, such as trying to find your path in life, or even a spiritual question, such as the order to the universe. Whatever question you choose, a focus crystal can help direct your ideas to a more streamlined train of thought, leading you toward something truly enlightening.

Specific Energies

Even if you are not looking for an answer to a specific question, you might want to harness a more specific type of energy in your meditation. Meditating can be an intimidating practice for a lot of people since it requires total concentration. It can be easy for your mind to wander, especially if you are not an experienced meditator. Thus, bringing certain crystals in can help you really focus your meditation energy, resulting in a more concentrated meditation practice. Using crystals to guide your feelings and thoughts in a certain direction is one of the best ways you can incorporate them into your practice.

Deepen Connections

When you use crystals in your meditation practice, you have the ability to deepen your meditative process and draw stronger connections between your spiritual practices. You can see how your relationship with crystals can echo in your relationship with your meditation practices and see how this symbiosis informs both. Creating this connection allows you to see the higher aspects of spirituality and the core aspects of spiritual practice as well as how many of these practices are attempting to access the same universal energy. You can even take this a step further and start incorporating astrological practices, numerology, or Tarot into your crystal meditation, perhaps choosing certain phases of the moon or days of the week to meditate to enhance the experience. All spiritual practices are inherently connected, and practicing them together is a powerful way to start seeing the higher plane that they are all reaching for.

Understand Your Crystals

More than just using crystals to enhance your meditation, meditation can also help you understand your crystals more deeply. Taking special time with each of your crystals is an amazing way to really dive into the very specific way each crystal works for you. This is especially effective if you really go one crystal at a time with your meditation. When wearing crystals or keeping them around the house, you aren't really spending intentional, focused time with them. However, when you are sitting individually with one particular crystal, then you can really notice the way it affects you. Observe yourself a little during this meditation practice. How does the crystal make you feel? What thoughts come to mind? Is it making you feel relaxed or energized? You can even write a short reflection after this meditation if you want to record your experience. You might find that you end up wanting to do this reflection every time you buy a new crystal so you can really get to know how it affects you!

What Crystals Should You Use?

If you are going to try different kinds of meditation, then you should experiment with different crystals. Focus crystals tend to be popular for meditation since they help you to streamline your ideas. However, you can choose different kinds of crystals for this practice, not just focus ones. It all depends on what your goals for the meditation session are. If you intend to have a purely relaxing session, then bringing along crystals that will help with that relaxation is prudent. However, if you want to dig deep into your soul, then you will need crystals that focus on truth and revelations. Or perhaps you are interested in manifestation meditation, in which case you should choose a crystal that relates to the facet of your life in which you are trying to manifest. Basically, the crystals you choose should correspond to the goals you have for your meditation practice. In Chapter 17, when I list all the pertinent crystals, you should consider how each one can be used during meditation. Reflect on your meditation goals, as well as the crystals you personally connect with, and you will be able to choose the right one that will fit your meditation practice perfectly.

How to Use Crystals in Your Meditation Practice

So, now that you know why you should use crystals for meditation and what crystals are best to use, you can start learning how to use them. The long and short of it is that there is no one way to integrate crystals into your existing meditation practice. It's all up to the way you prefer to meditate and your relationship with crystals. Some people feel the effects of crystals very strongly and thus can't be too close to them without becoming overwhelmed. On the other hand, many people feel that they need to have their crystals very close to them in order to feel any effect at all. In another vein, there is also the issue of parts of the body, or chakras, where you feel your crystals have the strongest effect. In order to harness a crystal's meditative power, you need to find the method that works best for you. There is no one way of doing so, but there are some established methods that might be a good jumping-off point for you. In this section, I will share some of these methods so you can begin to explore the ways crystal healing can be incorporated into your meditation practice.

The Holding Method

The simplest way to meditate with crystals is to simply hold one while you meditate. This is best to use with focus crystals when you are attempting to channel a particular thought or feeling through your crystal. When you hold a crystal, you want to center its power and channel your thoughts through it. Sit down or stand, depending on what you prefer, and hold the crystal out in front of you. Concentrate on the crystal and how it feels in your hand. Whether or not you have your eyes open, make sure you know where it is in space. Then, think about the topic you are meditating on very carefully, concentrating on the crystal at the same time. This should help your energies work together well and channel the questions through your crystals. Even if you aren't using a focus crystal, the holding method requires you to channel your energies through your hands and the crystal inside of them. If you are intending the crystal to have more of an effect on you, try to feel the ebb and flow coming from your palms up your arms and radiating throughout your body. This way, you should be able to really concentrate on the energy of that one crystal, either channeling your thoughts through its prism or allowing its energy into your body.

The Chakra Method

As I talked about in Chapter 3 with chakras, crystal practice is linked with the chakras of the body, so you might want to incorporate those concepts into your practice. This meditation method will involve concentrating on a certain part of your body and the crystal it is associated with. To choose a crystal for your chakra meditation process, you should use three frameworks: crystals associated with the particular thing you are manifesting or unblocking, crystals associated with the chakra you are targeting, and of course, crystals you personally connect with. If you are able to find the crystal that fits all these criteria, you will be well on your way to unblocking your chakras and creating balance throughout your body.

The method by which you should use crystals to target your chakras during meditation involves lying facedown and placing crystals strategically along your back at your central chakra points. So, if you are targeting your root chakra, you would place the crystal over your tailbone, and if you are targeting your heart chakra, you would place the crystal right between your shoulder blades, and so on. You might need a friend or masseuse to aid you with this practice. Lie there for as long as you think you need to and really concentrate on that part of your body and the crystal's impact on it. Try to feel that same ebb and flow entering that part of your body as a loosening agent. At the same time, you can also concentrate on issues pertinent to that chakra. For example, if you are targeting your sacral chakra with your crystals lying on your lower back, reflect on some issues you might be insecure about and feel them being cleansed and leaving your body. You'll likely find that this targeted practice will help you with more specific problems that relate to clear facets of your life. Crystals can be a very effective way to open up blocked chakras.

The Surrounding Method

For those who are more sensitive to crystal power or who want to incorporate a wider array of crystals into their practice, you can try the surrounding method. The surrounding method involves laying your crystals out in a formation around your person as you meditate. The formation, the amount and type of crystals, and the placement of

Monique Wagner

each individual crystal are all up to you. The advantage of this method is that it welcomes many different crystals so that you can mix and match, creating a wonderful variety of energies. However, you should be wary that this benefit can also be a drawback as mixing too many crystals together can be challenging and potentially dangerous for the inexperienced crystal user. Combining two incompatible or hyperintense crystals can create a confusing meditation experience. Since most people want meditation to be relaxing, clarifying, or even rejuvenating, creating conflicting energies is probably the last thing you want to do. Thus, you should make sure to do your research and learn about the crystals you are using and their effect on one another.

To perform your meditation using the surrounding method, you can incorporate some of the above techniques. For example, you can use the concentration of the holding method by selecting a particular crystal to place in front of you and concentrate your energy on. You can also incorporate chakras into the surrounding method by placing certain crystals strategically to match up with your chakras. You can achieve this either by lying down and placing the crystals around you at chakra points or by hanging your crystals at chakra points while sitting up. Combining these methods can help you really enhance the surrounding method and can even be a good modification for those who find touching crystals to be too intense.

The Yoga Method

Another method of meditating with crystals is to incorporate them into a meditative yoga practice. Just as there are different kinds of meditation and crystal practices, there are also many different kinds of yoga practice. However, if you are practicing more meditation-driven yoga,

88

then you might want to consider incorporating some crystals. You can use the surrounding method by placing crystals around the area where you want to do your yoga practice or even wear your crystals while you practice your yoga. This method can also cross over with the chakra method, especially if you are trying to unblock a certain chakra and want to use its corresponding crystal to do so. No matter the spiritual practice, they can often be intertwined to help benefit you on your spiritual journey.

Pillar 4:
Preparation

Moving away from the purposes and possible applications of your crystals, we will now get into the core of crystal practice: the actual preparation and use of your crystals. You might not know it, but preparation is actually a huge part of using crystals. Treating your crystals properly is integral for them to be effective. In this pillar, I will be showing you all the essential ways you need to prepare your crystals.

Chapter 11:
Cleansing Your Crystals

The first step of the preparation process is to cleanse your crystals. You may not realize it, but the outside world can actually have a huge effect on your crystals. Similar to how your crystals impose their vibrations on the rest of the world, so too does the world impose vibrations on your crystals. These other vibrations can have a great influence on how your crystals work and can sometimes completely decimate their intended purpose. Cleansing is especially important to do when you first purchase your crystals. They have either been in a store, being touched by many people every day, or in a shipping warehouse, where they may have been tossed from person to person. All those people had their own energies that they were bringing and which might have had an effect on your crystals. You don't want to be encountering all those people's energies when you engage in your own crystal practice. Thus, cleansing is essential when you first purchase your crystals, no matter what. But it's not just at the beginning that they need to be cleansed. Your crystals are exposed to many different energies throughout the time you are using them. Whether it's the people you encounter while you are wearing your crystals, people who are invited into your home, or simply your own different energies rubbing off on them, your crystals should be cleaned regularly to make sure that they are always fresh and ready to use to their full potential.

Now, what do I mean by cleaning? It's not a physical cleaning, although you can always do that too. No, what I am talking about is a spiritual cleansing of the crystal's vibrations. You can think of this as a kind of reset, like restoring your laptop to factory mode or clearing a hard drive. All the debris and bugs that have accumulated in the crystal's vibrations are wiped clean and you can start fresh. You're probably wondering how this is done since there is no clear physical process to "wipe" a crystal. Well, I am here to help. There are a few different methods for cleansing crystals, all of which bring their own qualities to the table. The method you choose will be up to you and your crystal practice as well as the degree of cleansing you are going for. In this chapter, I will outline for you the fundamentals of crystal cleansing so you can ensure that you always have properly reset crystals.

Method #1: Plain Water

Sometimes, you just have to cleanse your crystals the old-fashioned way: with plain water. Water is the root cleansing material, the substance that humans and animals alike have washed themselves with for millions of years. For cleansing crystals specifically, running water is essential. Bathing your crystal in a tub of standing water will keep its old vibrations surrounding it. Running water, on the other hand, is able to completely wash away any negative energy. You want your water to be cold and free-flowing for this purpose. For the best results, you should try using a natural water source, such as a stream. This will imbue your crystal with energy from the earth. However, if you don't have access to a natural river or stream, then you can use tap water, but make sure it is flowing freely. To achieve a proper cleanse, hold your stones under the running water for at least a full minute. This technique is great for a quick cleanse to breathe some fresh life into your crystals.

Method #2: Salt Water

For a deeper, more chemical cleanse, you can use salt water. While fresh water is associated with the clean mountain springs of the earth, salt water is associated with the deep and powerful oceans. Salt water has natural disinfecting and purifying qualities, which is why doctors will often prescribe it for infected wounds or mouth sores. You can also use this purifying quality to cleanse your crystals. This kind of cleanse is for a more deeply disrupted stone as opposed to running water which really only cleans the surface. The technique to cleanse your crystals with salt water is to submerge them for at least a few hours, if not a few days. This will allow the salt water to fully penetrate your stone to its core and allow all the unwanted vibrations to seep out. You might want to perform a post-cleansing rinse using the above method with fresh water, just to ensure everything is washed off and you don't have any negative vibrations or salt water residue still clinging to your crystal. As with fresh water, you will have the best results with natural salt water. Obviously, this is not really feasible for anyone who doesn't live in a coastal location, so you can make your own using salt and water. If you are landlocked but still very serious about using natural seawater, you can always order some online and have it delivered to you. However, salted water will still be suitable. For a more natural touch, you can use a raw salt source, such as Himalayan pink salt or sea salt. This technique gives your crystals a deep, thorough cleanse that will completely reset the way that they heal.

Method #3: Rice

Have you ever heard the advice about putting a waterlogged phone into a bowl of rice to try to save it? That technique is based on the fact that rice has natural absorption properties. Rice is naturally porous, so it tends to soak up any moisture around it. Crystal healers, however, will use rice to not only absorb water but negative energy as well. Instead of soaking into your crystals as with salt water, rice instead draws the negative effects out of your crystals. The method of soaking is done in almost exactly the same way as with salt water. You place your crystals in a bowl of rice and soak them for at least 24 hours. This should be enough time to pull out any negative energy that you don't want in your crystals. Rice can do wonders for drawing any conflicting vibrations out of your crystals and creating a fresh environment.

Method #4: Sunlight

Besides water and grain, the other life-giving element on this earth is the sun. Anyone who has stepped outside on a beautiful day knows how rejuvenating just a few hours of sunlight can be. It can make you feel like a big solar panel, having your batteries recharged by the warm light. Well, the same actually goes for your crystals. Even though it might not seem like much, exposing your crystals to a healthy amount of sunlight can actually be a powerful cleansing agent. Putting your crystals outside on a sunny day in an exposed area can give them the heat and light cleanse they need to reset.

Method #5: Moonlight

As an alternative to cleansing with sunlight, you can also soak your crystals in moonlight. Moonlight is simply a reflection of the sun's light, so it has already been filtered and subdued. Cleansing with moonlight is less harsh than cleansing with sunlight, but it is equally important. If you want a softer, more mystical approach to cleansing with light, moonlight can be a great option. Of course, you can always time it so that your crystals get a little bit of both. Try to find a sunny day followed by a full moon so that you get the best possible effect for your crystals.

Chapter 12:
Charging Your Crystals

Once your crystals are nice and cleansed, you can now start charging them. Charging your crystals is an integral part of the process of infusing them with energy. As much as crystals bring their own energy to the table, their energy comes from a connection to the earth. Just like batteries, and even people, they need to reconnect with a power source every once in a while to replenish their energy. When you are embarking on your crystal journey, you will need to learn how to charge your crystals in order to maintain their energy throughout your time with them. All the best crystal practitioners regularly charge their crystals and swear by some of their favorite methods. In this chapter, I will teach you all about the process of charging crystals so that you, too, can participate in this important aspect of crystal healing. First, I will give you an overview of the difference between charging and cleansing. Next, I will describe a general timeline and schedule for when you should give your crystals a good charge. And finally, I will enlighten you about some of the ways in which you can effectively charge your crystals. By the end of the chapter, you should have a solid grasp of the process for charging your crystals and be ready to start doing it yourself.

What Is Crystal Charging?

So, what exactly is going on when you charge your crystal? And what is exactly the difference between charging and cleansing? Well, the main difference is output versus input. When you cleanse your crystals, you are removing negative energy from them, allowing them to recalibrate their vibrations and come to a more balanced state. When you charge your crystals, on the other hand, you are imbuing them with positive or energizing vibrations. Though crystals retain their natural vibrations indefinitely, exposing them to positive energies can do a lot for their productivity. Thus, charging is like giving your crystal vibrations a boost. It's like flavoring a cast-iron skillet. The skillet might work on its own, but taking proper care of it—washing it with sea salt and allowing flavors to soak into it—can really enhance its performance. Charging your crystals gives them a recalibration in a different way than cleansing does by infusing them with energy rather than removing energy from them.

When Should You Charge Your Crystals?

So, we know that you should cleanse crystals when you first get them and when you feel they have been exposed to excessive negative or conflicting energies. These experiences can confuse your crystals and cause their energies to become imbalanced. But when do you charge your crystals? Well, we can think of the relationship between cleansing and charging as being like washing and moisturizing your skin. After you take a shower—washing your skin—you want to moisturize your body to restore some of the hydration lost during washing. Because cleaning with soap can strip the body's natural oils, adding moisturizer afterward is essential to help your skin retain moisture. The concept is similar for cleaning and charging crystals. If you have recently cleaned your crystals, they will be much more vulnerable than before as they have been completely stripped down to their natural vibrations. Thus, they could use a boost to help recalibrate their energy. For this reason, it's a good idea to combine your charging schedule with your cleansing schedule, doing one after the other. This way, your crystals will get a dual energy replenishment and be able to come back as strong as possible.

How to Charge Crystals

Now that you know why and when you should charge your crystals, we need to talk about how to do so. As with cleansing, there are many ways in which you can charge your crystals. Many of these substances will have slightly different effects on your crystals, so you should make sure that you know the specific qualities of everything that you are using to charge each crystal. Similar to choosing the crystal yourself, you should make sure you are in tune with the vibrations you are giving to your crystals. In this section, I will outline some of the most common methods and materials people use to charge their crystals.

Burial

Crystals come from the earth. It's no wonder, then, that they draw so much energy from it. It is the ground that first imbues your crystals with all their potent energy, drawing all their vibrations out of the very core of the earth. When we mine them, we sever that connection. Yes, we are still able to harness the powers of the crystal continuously after this, but we must remember that it is the ground that formed the crystal and gave it its natural vibrations. When you restore this connection, even for just a few hours, you give the crystal a boost from its natural home that it needs in order to really shine.

The general method for charging your crystal through burial is very simple. All you have to do is dig a hole anywhere in the ground. This could be in your backyard or even a safe public space that is very secluded where the crystal is not likely to be stolen. If you don't have access to a burial place in the ground, you can try burying your crystal in a large potted plant to simulate the experience of being buried in the ground, but this does mean that your crystal won't have access to the strong earth connection of being buried directly in the ground. For another modification, if you have a crystal that is apt to get dirty and is hard to physically clean, such as a very jagged one, you can put it in a protective container. However, you should know that burying your crystal bare will have the most powerful effects. For the best results, you should leave your crystals buried underground for at least a week each time you recharge them. This will allow their temperature to fully regulate and absorb all the vibrations of the earth. You can leave them there for less time, but you might not get the full effect you want. Burying a crystal in the ground allows it to reconnect to its roots (literally) and restore some of its most primal vibrations.

Singing Bowls

Vibrations are a huge part of crystals, as we have discussed at length throughout this book; vibrations are also a core aspect of sound. Sound might not seem like something powerful, since you cannot see or touch it, but it can actually have an immense impact on your crystals. Now, almost any sound can affect your crystals. Your own voice even has an effect. You can try singing or chanting to your crystals to try and align them with your energy. These strategies are very popular and have proven effective. But one of the most common ways people use sound to charge their crystals is with singing bowls. These are the round metal bowls you can find at most spirituality stores that have a stick that goes along with them, sometimes resembling a mortar and pestle. When you drag the stick along the outer edge of the bowl, you create a beautiful sound. These bowls are not just used for crystals but to generally help people with their vibrations. The sound has a powerful quality that can really ignite energy. For this reason, singing bowls are absolutely perfect for charging crystals.

You can charge crystals using singing bowls by sounding them in the vicinity of your crystals. The closer your crystals are to the sound, the more intense the effect will be on them. If you have small enough crystals or a big enough bowl, you can even put your crystals inside the bowl to get the maximum effect. Some crystal healers refer to this as giving your crystals a "sound bath." Bathing your crystals in the beautiful vibrations of your singing bowl is a powerful way to charge them. This is especially true for those who already incorporate singing bowls into their existing spiritual practice. For those people, sound baths are one of the ideal methods of charging your crystals as they will help align all the vibrations of your different spiritual practices.

Incense

Another one of the senses you can use to charge your crystals is smell. There are so many herbs and spices with different qualities that can be useful for charging. Look at the incense you normally use and evaluate how it might be compatible with your crystals. Try to match different kinds of incense with crystals that are also attuned to that particular quality. If you are able to do this, then you will be able to charge your crystals with the exact kind of energy that will really make them sparkle.

There are a few distinct ways you can charge your crystals with incense. One method involves burning the incense and then allowing your crystals to pass through the smoke. This exposes them to the vibrations in the smoke, coating them with a thin film of residue. This can help the healing effects of the incense truly soak into the crystals. The other method involves smudging or rubbing the soot from the incense smoke on your crystals. Both of these methods involve coating your crystals with the incense residue, which is an important way to really allow the two energies to contact one another. Some popular types of incense to use include herbs or pure incense like lavender, sandalwood, and jasmine. When you do this technique right, you will be infusing your crystal with certain energies, just like with singing bowls.

Salt

If you want to infuse your crystals with another crystal, you can actually use salt! Technically, salt is chemically a crystal. It is not generally used in crystal practice, except perhaps Himalayan pink salt, but it has a strong relationship to your spiritual crystals because of this quality. Thus, you can actually use salt to charge the crystals in your practice.

We talked back in the last chapter about using salt water, which is water infused with salt, for cleansing. But for charging, you need something a little bit more powerful. Soaking your crystals in a bowl of salt, especially a more natural salt, can infuse them with all sorts of energies. Just like burying your crystals in the ground, immersing your crystals in salt reconnects them with their roots and allows them to exchange energies with other crystals.

Human Breath

Believe it or not, you also have strong spiritual energy and vibrations that can really rub off on your crystals! Just being around your crystals is inherently charging to them since your presence asserts your vibrations onto them. If you own crystals that you wear or otherwise interact with a lot, then you are already infusing them with your vibrations. But if you are actively charging your crystals, then you will want to make sure that they have as much exposure to your vibrations as possible. When we talk about human vibrations and auras, we mean a lot of things. Heartbeat, nervous system, breathing rhythms—all these things contribute to your overall aura frequency. Since it's hard to expose your crystals to the former two, many crystal healers use the latter in order to create a strong connection between their own vibrations and their crystals'. Breathing directly on your crystals exposes them not only to the rhythm of your breathing but also to the natural vibrations of your voice box. You can also try singing directly into your crystals to get the maximum vibration effect. This technique charges your crystals with powerful vibrations and ensures that they are strongly connected to you and your body's particular aura.

Connect Them With Your Spiritual Guides

If you are very embedded in the spiritual community, then you will likely have your own spiritual guides. These are figures, such as gods or astrological entities, who you feel you have a strong connection to and who you look to for guidance in your spiritual life. Many of the techniques we have talked about in this chapter focus heavily on connection. These techniques help you to form links between different aspects of your spiritual life and create pathways that will help you on your journey toward spiritual unity. If you are able to link your spiritual guides with your crystals, charging them with the right kind of energy for you, then you will be further enriching your spiritual web and creating strong connections all around.

Chapter 13:
Programming Your Crystals

The third major step before using your crystals is to program them. Programming is the natural progression from cleansing and charging. When you charge your crystals, you are infusing them with energy and boosting their abilities to serve their natural purpose. Programming, however, is a more focused kind of charging. If you think of charging as charging up your laptop, programming is like setting your desktop picture and downloading the software you want to use. While some of the charging methods I talked about in the previous chapter are helpful to steer your crystals toward your intention, programming is about directly stating your intention and setting your crystals on the exact path. In this chapter, I will lead you through the process of programming your crystals so that you can make sure they are on the best path of intentionality. First, I will give you the general definition and parameters of crystal programming. Then, I will explain some of the distinctive benefits of programming your crystals. And finally, I will show you a few of the many methods you can use to program your crystals toward the purposes you want them to serve. By the end of this chapter, you should have some very purposefully programmed crystals!

What Is Crystal Programming?

So, we know that crystal programming is all about setting your crystals toward specific intentions, but how exactly does that work? Well, programming your crystals is all about setting intentions. When you go to meditate, you likely already have an intention in your mind. You want to recharge, reflect on some ideas, or let go of your anxieties. Well, it's the same with crystals. Before you start using your crystals, you need to really set your intentions with them. What are you really using your crystals for? What kind of energies are you looking to bring into your life with them? What are the energies you are hoping they will help you banish? Where do you see your crystal journey taking you? Toward enlightenment about the higher things in life? Toward the kind of life you want to have? Toward a deeper connection with the universe and others? Considering all these important questions will greatly help you to program your crystals in the direction that is right for you.

Crystal programming also relates to the material qualities of your crystals, meaning that you have the ability to program your crystals with material conditions as well as with intentions. Some of the charging methods I talked about in the last chapter relate to specific things, but that was mostly just with alignment and forging connections between your spiritual practices. The methods outlined in this chapter will focus on more specific ways to guide your crystals in a certain direction. They will infuse your crystals with a particular quality which will allow you to focus the natural qualities of your crystals toward the exact use you are intending them for. In other words, programming is a more precise version of charging, one being revving up your engine and the other setting your course.

Benefits of Crystal Programming

There are many ways programming can completely revamp your crystal experience. You might have had exceptional experiences with crystals so far and can certainly go on using them without necessarily programming them every single time you use them, but you will assuredly get better and more focused results if you do program them. However, you will not get your desired results if you are attempting to go against the natural properties of the crystal. Stating your intentions should always be a narrowing-down process. You should consider your intentions before you even buy your crystals, and then you should continue to narrow down as you go. Trying to make a relaxation crystal into a manifesting crystal will only mean that you aren't getting what you want and are confusing the crystal's energy. As long as you are able to thoroughly match the crystal's qualities to your intentions, you will easily be able to program them to the intentions you have in mind.

Crystal Programming Methods

As with cleansing and charging, there are many ways you can program your crystals. Some of these ways will be more effective with certain types of crystals than with others. Certain methods will also be more effective with certain types of intentions than others, especially if you have very specific plans for your crystals. In this section, we will explore some of the most common methods people use to program their crystals. Some of these methods will involve pure manifestation on your part, while others will require specific ceremonies to be conducted. It all depends on what you feel is right for you and your crystal.

Manifestation

The clearest way to really program your crystals properly is to incorporate them into your manifestation process. Hold them while you are manifesting or meditating, and try to really link the thoughts going through your mind and the crystal you are holding in your hand. Visualization is a very important part of this process. Think about the thing you are trying to manifest in your life. Is it love? Creative inspiration? Money? Whatever it is, you need to connect with it. But connecting to it doesn't just mean thinking about the thing itself but rather how it specifically fits into your life. Think about the exact way in which you would experience the things you want and clearly visualize an image of your life with this newfound thing. If you do this while deeply connecting with your crystal, then you will be able to actually manifest what you want as well as program your crystal at the same time.

Chakra Method

Back in Chapter 3, we talked about how crystals relate to the chakras. There are often crystals that correspond to different chakras, and crystals can even help you to unblock or open up some of your chakras. But did you know you can also use your chakras to program your crystals? Because crystals are heavily connected to manifestation, the best chakra to use is actually your third eye chakra. This chakra is connected to your far-reaching goals and life plan. If you use this chakra to program your crystals, then you will forge a strong connection between these long-term plans and your chakras. The exact way in which you can accomplish this is to lie down and place your crystal of choice over your third eye chakra. Then, you can practice some of the same manifestation and visualization techniques listed above. You can think of this method as a sort of elevated version of the manifestation technique, using the specificity of the third eye chakra to help you guide your intentions toward your crystal's energy.

Crystal Grids

Another important method you can use to program your crystals is to actually use other crystals. Crystals obviously have strong vibration patterns that both affect and are affected by other vibration patterns. So, it follows that crystals are able to be influenced by one another. Your crystals, especially if they have different vibrations or are for different purposes, can have a massive impact on each other. They can pick up on each others' vibration patterns and exchange energies. Creating this symbiosis between crystals is a very important aspect of programming them, especially if this is a group of crystals that you intend to use in conjunction with one another. Just like syncing your crystals up with your own energies and the rest of your spiritual practices, syncing your crystals up with each other is also crucial. Plus, if you sync your crystal combinations properly, you can actually create a more dynamic effect than you might have had otherwise.

So, how do you sync your crystals? Well, one of the most popular methods of doing so is to use something called a "crystal grid." A crystal grid is essentially an arrangement of crystals designed so that they can feed off of one another's energies. You can use crystal grids to program and just practice in general. Crystal grids do all of what I listed above: construct a relationship between your crystals and help you to gather multiple energies in one place for a more powerful crystal healing session. When you use a crystal grid to program, you are subtly creating a dynamic and hierarchy among your crystals. You are introducing them to one another, setting the precedent for the way they will be used in tandem in the future.

The arrangement of the crystals is, of course, paramount when it comes to a crystal grid. Most crystal grids are constructed as a circle, with one "dominant" crystal in the center and the other crystals surrounding it. However, you can decide what arrangement suits you best. If there is a particular shape or pattern that you feel speaks to you spiritually, such as a triangle or a star, then feel free to use that shape. Most shapes will have a crystal placed so that forms some sort of center or peak. Where you place each crystal within the hierarchy will have a great impact on the way the crystal functions in regard to the others. If placed in a strong position, this crystal's vibrations might have dominance over the other crystals, thus setting a definitive precedent for the vibrations of the collection as a whole. For this reason, you should choose which crystal goes in this position wisely, picking the one you feel the strongest connection with and the one you feel has the most bearing on your intentions. This way, you will charge all of your crystals with your favorite one, aligning them with your chosen energy.

Chapter 14:
Setting Your Intention

In order to use crystals effectively, you have to know what you are using them for. You don't want to go manifesting the wrong things. Even if you are aware of the vague ideas you want to manifest, you might not be specific enough in those intentions. Manifesting vague things with your crystals is almost as bad as manifesting the wrong things since you are basically not giving your crystals the proper directions. You might find that you end up in a "be careful what you wish for" kind of situation, where you are in a negative version of your intended manifested purpose. For this reason, setting your intentions properly is one of the most important aspects of crystal use. In this chapter, we are going to step back from hard crystal knowledge and discuss your reasoning for using crystals. I will take you through the step-by-step process of ironing out your clear intentions for your crystal practice and creating a plan for how you are going to use your crystals.

Step 1: Determine the Facet of Life You Are Manifesting

It's always good to narrow your ideas down before coming up with something major. When you are embarking on a journey of manifestation, you need to start by identifying where in your life you are trying to manifest positive energy. Is it in your love life, your professional life, your creative life, your friendships, or something else? This area doesn't necessarily have to be an area in which you are extremely deficient. For example, many people who are working in their dream field still have goals and aspirations related to their careers, and many people in happy marriages still pray for longevity in their relationships. Thus, the facet of life that you are manifesting in can be any facet in which you have goals, hopes, dreams, or aspirations. Anywhere you feel like you could have more or go further can be an area for manifesting. You might also want to manifest in multiple areas of your life at the same time. If that is the case, you should still follow these steps individually for each one. For the purposes of this step, you should decide what category you are trying to manifest within.

Step 2: Determine Where You Are Now

The next step of the process is to take a good hard look at what that facet of your life looks like now. As much as many happy people still want to manifest, you might also be experiencing a hard time. Knowing how you currently feel in that facet of your life will be integral in figuring out what exactly you are trying to manifest. Ask yourself this question: "What do I feel is lacking in this part of my life?" It might be everything. For example, you might be single and desperate for a relationship, and therefore you are simply lacking the presence of romance in your life. Or, you might already be in a relationship but experiencing a rough patch with your partner, so you are lacking some of the more nuanced aspects of love. Career-wise, you might be happy in your job but feel like you are due for a promotion and are therefore feeling somewhat of a lack of professional appreciation. Or, alternatively, you might be in a completely dead-end job and feel like you are lacking any professional satisfaction. Whatever your degree or type of deprivation, you need to identify the missing piece that is driving you to want to manifest change in that area.

Step 3: Determine Where You Want to Be in the Short and Long Term

Once you have determined your current state of affairs, you need to really investigate what you want them to turn into. Just identifying your lack is not enough; you have to identify what you want to take its place. Failing to do so might result in you manifesting the wrong kind of energy to replace it. So, for example, if you are single and want to be in a relationship, you can't just manifest for the alleviation of your loneliness—you have to manifest for the actual type of relationship you are seeking. Otherwise, your spiritual guides won't have a clear idea and you could end up in an unhealthy or unsatisfactory relationship because you failed to really define the details of what you actually want. This is where you start to form the basis of your manifestation. You are creating clear aspirations out of your dissatisfaction.

One important element of this step is to consider the difference between the near future and the more distant future. Most goals will have both components to them, with the short-term goals merely being stepping stones to your longer-term goals. So, in regards to your romantic life, your long-term goal might be to be happily married with kids, but your short-term goal is simply to get a date. In the professional world, your short-term goal might be a promotion, whereas your long-term goal is to become CEO of your company. All of these goals are important to consider. So, when you are looking at how you want your deficiency to be transformed, you have to think about how you want it to be addressed immediately as well as down the road. This will give you two distinctive visions to concentrate on as you move forward in your manifesting journey.

Step 4: Create a Mood Board

After you've really dug deep into what your goals are, you need to start visualizing them more carefully. One of the most popular ways to visualize goals for your life and yourself is to create a mood board. Conventionally, a mood board is a collection of photographs or other images representing an idealized version of what you want. Think of a mood board as a bulletin board for your future. You can add clothes you would like to wear, places you would like to live or visit, professions you would like to have, and so forth. They don't have to represent the exact things you want, but their purpose is to give you a visual representation of the type of life you want. When people plan their weddings, they will often create mood boards with images of things like dresses, decorations, food, cakes, and other wedding-related items. They won't necessarily have those exact flower garlands or centerpieces, but they will have a clear visual guide to show a wedding planner so that they can create something similar. This is what you are going to do for your future self.

Mood boards help you visualize the life you want more clearly, showing you the life you could have if you achieve your goals. Since manifestation relies so heavily on visualization, mood boards help you to create that mental picture of what your future life is going to look like. That being said, a mood board does not necessarily need to be completely visual. You can simply collect things that inspire you. So, if you are looking to become an entrepreneur, you might not find it helpful to create a picture collage of people in business suits, but you might find it helpful to create a list of entrepreneurs who inspire you or a YouTube playlist of some talks about starting a business. These items aren't necessarily pictures per se, but they still give you something definitive to look at in order to help your manifestation brain visualize what you want.

Step 5: Connect Your Desires to Your Core Self

In psychology, there is a dichotomy known as intrinsic motivation versus extrinsic motivation. Extrinsic motivation is motivation that is unrelated to the actual task at hand but instead is based on the pursuit of a material reward, such as a paycheck or a prize. Intrinsic motivation, on the other hand, is the desire to do something for its own sake, reaping pure satisfaction from accomplishment itself. So, if you bake because you love creating interesting combinations of flavors and get satisfaction out of completing the task well, that would be intrinsic motivation, whereas if you bake because you work in a bakery and need to make your weekly paycheck, that is extrinsic motivation. Even though some extrinsic motivation is effective, many psychologists believe that intrinsic motivation is actually more powerful. When you connect the task you are doing with your deepest desires and values, then you will be more likely to accomplish it well because it's the accomplishment itself that is of value.

When you get to the manifestation stage, you really need to be able to find intrinsic motivation for the goal you have set. This is important to do for two reasons. The first reason is that your goals will be more focused and easier to achieve. If you want a promotion because you want to make a higher salary versus because you want to make a difference in a way that only the higher position can really achieve, then you might not get as far. The other reason you should try to find as much intrinsic motivation as possible is that, for manifestation to be effective, you need to really believe it at the core of your being. The crystals respond to your innermost vibrations. If the desire isn't vibrating at the very core of your body, the crystals will not be able to truly pick up on it, even if you are screaming it in your conscious mind. In order to really achieve results with your crystal manifestation, you have to ensure that your goals are strongly aligned with your innermost values.

Pillar 5:
Care

So, you've prepared your crystals, you've set your intentions, and you've been able to manifest great things. You are truly reaping the benefits of all your amazing crystals have to offer. But now you need to take a bit of a step back and ask yourself what you are offering to your crystals. By now, you really understand that crystals are like living things. They are rife with vibrations, life, and energy. You can't just treat them like inanimate objects. As I talked about in the chapter on cleansing, crystals are very susceptible to outside influences, and vice versa. If you don't take care of them properly, your crystals can easily become misaligned, or worse, misalign other things too. In this pillar, we will be focusing on how to properly care for your crystals. This is an extremely important aspect of working with crystals, helping you to give back to your crystals and treat them right after they have given so much to you.

Chapter 15:
Storing Crystals

The way you store your crystals can have a huge impact on how they work. You can think of crystal storage as kind of like your crystals' off time. This is their time to relax, recharge, and rest for the next time you want to use them. But storing them is not quite as simple as that. Where you choose to store a crystal can have an effect on the crystal as well as the space. The combination of crystals that can be stored together is also an important complexity to acknowledge. You might also be interested in how long you should store your crystals. All these questions and more are important to investigate. In this chapter, I will guide you through proper storing practices for your crystals, helping you to create a healthy environment in which your crystals can rest in between healing sessions.

What Your Crystals Need Protection From

As we stated above, your crystals are very open to outside influences. You saw in the previous few chapters how many different influences and elements have the ability to strongly affect your crystals. Any kind of vibration can completely alter the way your crystals work. This is good if you are trying to influence them in a certain way since it allows you to really customize your crystals to your specific needs, but it is not good in the sense that, if gone uncontrolled, your crystals can pick up a lot of outside influences without you realizing it. When you are storing your crystals, there are a few things that you need to be concerned with. In this section, I will give you a list of the major things you need to keep your crystals away from during their storage period in order to protect them from these influences.

Light

As we talked about in the chapter on cleansing, crystals can actually be greatly affected by light. Sunlight and moonlight in particular are very activating to crystals. If your crystal is exposed to natural sunlight or moonlight without being properly regulated, these can have an excess influence on its vibrations and possibly cause it to go out of whack. On another note, some crystals can be physically damaged from too much sunlight. Have you ever removed a picture from the wall in a brightly lit room only to realize that the sun has faded the wallpaper over time and there is a much more saturated square under where the picture used to be? Well, if sunlight can have this effect on wallpaper, it can certainly have an effect on crystals. So, for both their physical and spiritual well-being, try to keep your crystals in a dark place when storing them.

Water

The other major influence on crystals is water. In the chapter on cleansing your crystals, I talked about how running water and salt water can significantly influence your crystals. While you do want to cleanse your crystals regularly, you also don't want them to be constantly exposed to water. As with light, this can have a destabilizing effect on their vibrations, so it is best to keep your crystals' water exposure very controlled. Likewise, water can also damage certain crystals physically. Water has a corrosive or erosive effect on rocks if they are exposed to it for too long, so make sure your crystals are not stored in any place where they could get wet or rained on, both for the sake of their vibrations as well as their physical integrity.

People

People have energies and vibrations that can actually affect a crystal's energy. This is why I advised you to cleanse your crystals after they come in contact with other people, especially the general public, because all of the energies they bring to the table will have an effect on your crystals. This is why you should make sure to store crystals in a space where they won't be consistently exposed to people. This will make sure that their vibrations are kept pure and uninfluenced by people. It is for this reason that many people don't keep their crystals displayed, at least not unless they are actively trying to influence that room. Keeping your crystals displayed can cause their vibrations to be disrupted, especially if that area is used frequently by a lot of people. So, keep your crystals in a space where they will have lots of privacy, such as a closet or secured drawer.

Each Other

And finally, your crystals can also have an effect on one another. In the last chapter, I talked about crystal grids and how they can be used for programming. They can influence each other's vibrations and thus change the nature of each other's healing abilities. Well, the same goes for storage. If you store two crystals together, they will have an influence on one another. Unless this is something you want, you should probably store your crystals as separately as possible. Even putting them in different compartments of a jewelry box is a good way to get a small amount of the separation that they need.

What Needs Protection From Your Crystals

On the other end of the spectrum, crystals also will influence other things with their vibrations. Again, you do want this in some capacity, but making sure that your crystals don't have any undue influence on yourself and the people and world around you is responsible. For this reason, you should not only be very careful about which crystals you wear around whom but also about where those crystals are when you're not wearing or using them. You might inadvertently be exposing your friends or family to powerful crystal vibrations that should really only be used consciously and in small doses. This is especially true for very powerful crystals or crystals that have transformative energy. These can be very disruptive to someone's life, so they need to be handled with care. Leaving them lying around can potentially cause a lot of problems. So, for example, you might accidentally leave your crystal storage kit in the guest room of your house only to have a guest stay over and unwittingly experience the effects of the crystals in the kit. Or, you might think it's safe to store crystals in your bedside table drawer but are actually being affected by them in your sleep. Crystal vibrations are very powerful, so make sure you store them wisely.

Pillar 6:
Directory

Throughout this book, I have talked at length about the various uses for crystals and how different types of crystals can correspond to all sorts of things, like chakras, astrological signs, ailments, and so on. But what are these specific crystals? What are the names of some of the crystals you can use and what is each one generally used for? I have thus far avoided mentioning any specific crystals, but in this pillar, I will finally be answering this question. Here, we will look at some actual crystals and the purposes they serve in crystal healing practice.

Chapter 16:
Crystal List

You're probably wondering what exact crystals you should be using for your practice. I've already given you some advice about how to choose crystals, such as to trust your intuition or to select based on your intentions, but now I will get into the different crystals and what they are best used for. In this chapter, you will find a list of some of the most commonly used crystals and a brief description of each one's various applications.

Clear Quartz

When you think of crystals, you are probably picturing clear quartz. Clear quartz looks like the archetypal crystal: It is a clear, glassy stone that shines with white light. It is easily the most common crystal you can buy in stores. Moreover, clear quartz is also extremely versatile. This crystal can be used in almost any kind of crystal practice as a key grounding or protection crystal. What people mainly use clear quartz for is banishing negative energy. It can be used for any chakra because of its versatility but is especially useful for the third eye and crown chakras, which deal with clarity.

Rose Quartz

As you might be able to guess from its name, rose quartz is a beautiful pink stone. It is generally connected to the world of romance, earning it the nickname "the love stone." Rose quartz is probably the second most common crystal after clear quartz. It generally deals with the more emotional aspects of life, helping you to connect with others and even humanity at large. It is also known as a de-stressing stone, helping you to ease some of those tight anxieties that can build up over time. Many people also connect the rose quartz to their feminine side, and it has even been known to regulate menstrual cycles. The chakra that corresponds to rose quartz is of course the heart chakra, which is responsible for the more interpersonal side of life.

Smoky Quartz

The final type of quartz I will talk about is smoky quartz. Smoky quartz is a very powerful crystal known for banishing negative energy from your life. This stone is known to work best alone as it is a very foundational crystal and has an extremely powerful independent energy, so it may not be the best choice for your crystal grid. It is generally considered to be a rebalancing stone and can help you let go of old or stale belief systems. Its corresponding chakra is the root chakra since this crystal has the power to both destabilize your core beliefs as well as to ground you in new ones to find a way forward. Between these three types of quartz, we have the bottom, the middle, and the top chakra covered. Many people like to have all three so they can deliberately target different chakra areas comprehensively.

Amethyst

Moving away from the transformative power of the smoky crystal, amethysts are a very low-key stone. They are thus also very common crystals for people to own. In fact, many people have amethysts purely for decoration because of their sparkly texture and gorgeous purple shade. Most people will use amethyst as a balancing crystal, helping them to restore peace to their lives. It is also very commonly used for chronic pain issues. The amethyst is associated with the crown chakra, helping you to balance and regulate all your body's systems.

Angelite

As its name suggests, angelite has strong celestial connections. Its coloring echoes this as well—a soft sky blue. This crystal is all about purifying. If you feel like you have a very cluttered life and are losing connections to the things that you believe in, angelite can help you clear away some of the debris and breathe some fresh air into your life. It is also a deeply calming crystal and is especially good at helping you sleep. Hanging or placing an angelite crystal near your bed at night can help you achieve a more serene sleep. The angelite crystal is associated with the higher three chakras, including the throat, third eye, and crown, connecting to its regulating and purifying powers.

Green Jade

One of the most popular crystals used in jewelry, the green jade crystal is a beautiful opaque green, suggesting serenity and earthiness even in its coloring. Green jade is one of the best crystals to use for meditation. It has a calming effect that can really take your meditation abilities to the next level. Its corresponding chakra is the heart chakra, which connects it also to the spheres of love and romance, even family. Use green jade to connect more deeply to others and your spiritual self.

Tiger's Eye

The tiger's eye crystal is a smoky brown crystal that evokes an earthy but mysterious tone. As you might gather from its name, this crystal really promotes boldness. It is a crystal that can help you find your courage in a given situation. It is also associated with creativity. If you feel like you are experiencing a creative block or are having trouble sharing your creative side with others, tiger's eye can really help with that. Its corresponding chakra is the sacral chakra, which connects to the confidence-building and creative energy of the stone.

Malachite

This stone is not for the faint of heart. Its dark green wavy patterns represent the depths of the sea and all the powerful, unknowable entities that lie down there. Malachite is typically used for transformation purposes. It has the power to really banish negative energy from your life but often from a place or in a way that you weren't expecting. You might find that after using this crystal you lose friendships or experience intense upheavals in your life. While these things might be alarming, they are necessary for your growth. Malachite balances the heart and throat chakras, connecting with the communication and interpersonal honesty this crystal promotes.

Black Onyx

Black onyx is one of the prototypical protection crystals. It is imperative for your life to retain its positive energies and move toward a purely positive existence and mindset. As with malachite, black onyx is mainly used to expel negative energy from your life. Although it is somewhat less potent, it can still be a dangerous crystal to use because of the amount of change it can bring. Again, expect to see toxic people leave your life abruptly and for other major changes to take place. The main difference between malachite and black onyx is their chakra connection as black onyx is linked with the root chakra. Fundamental changes in your life will usually take place with the black onyx.

Fluorite

If you are looking for clarity in your life, you will want to use fluorite. This aqua-colored crystal is perfect for seeing the world realistically. Some people describe using this crystal as like wiping the fog off their windshield, allowing them to see clearly for the first time. Fluorite is also all about living in the moment. It can help you stop dwelling on past experiences or fretting about future possibilities. In short, fluorite can bring a groundedness and realism to your life and is great for trying to work out problems. Fluorite is linked with the throat chakra due to its focus on clarity and honesty.

Lepidolite

If green jade and rose quartz are about connecting with other people, lepidolite is all about connecting with yourself. This dark purple stone is one of the most visually striking crystals on this list. It is a great tool if you want to start practicing some more rigorous self-love in your life. It can help you get in touch with your higher spiritual self, creating a powerful connection. This can also lead to you becoming a more naturally intuitive person, allowing yourself to listen to your subconscious mind a little more closely. This crystal is linked with the higher chakras, including the heart, third eye, and crown, connecting with its high spiritual significance.

Turquoise

Turquoise is often considered to be the stone of luck. It is a powerful tool for manifestation meditation. It helps to guide you toward your ideal life, the path you are best suited for in your highest life. When you use turquoise during meditation, you can more clearly visualize your deepest desires. In this way, it can actually help you learn a lot more about yourself than you might have previously thought possible. This stone is connected with the throat chakra and is often used to help people who have a fear of public speaking find their voice.

Black Tourmaline

This dark, charcoal-looking crystal is one of the subtler crystals of the bunch. This is a purifying crystal that can be used to ward off and clear the air of negative energies in your space. It is very slow to work, but the results it can get are spectacular. Because of this slowness, it is one of the best candidates for wearability or interior decoration, as we talked about back in Chapters 8 and 9. You might not notice a profound difference in your life right away after using black tourmaline, but if you keep it in your space long enough, over time you will realize how clean and pure your space feels, all thanks to this crystal's slowly powerful energy. This stone is connected with the root chakra, helping to connect you with your space and banish negative energy.

Green Calcite

If you have gone through trauma in your life or experienced debilitating mental health issues in relation to your self-image, then green calcite is the crystal for you. Green calcite can help you to process difficult events from your past, letting go of the possible negative feelings about yourself that they might have caused. This stone can also help rid you of limiting beliefs about yourself, such as insecurities telling you that you can't do something or that you're not good at certain things. This crystal is associated with the heart chakra, reverberating through yourself into all your relationships.

Pillar 7:
Healing

So, now that you know the most common crystals that are used in the practice, we can move on to how they are used for healing. Those who have had issues in their lives, whether psychological, physiological, or circumstantial, have likely searched for healing in some way. There are many avenues that you can take for healing, and not all of them are for everybody. Sometimes you find that you just can't find exactly what you're looking for in mainstream medical circles. You have to search for that kind of healing elsewhere. If you are someone who values holistic healing—that is, including both the mind and body in your healing process—then crystals can be a very helpful avenue for you. Crystals can bring all the faculties of the body together and help you to heal in a way that makes you feel good all over. In this pillar, we will look at the process of using crystals to heal yourself.

Chapter 17:
Healing

No matter what aspect of your life you are looking to heal, there is likely a crystal that can help you with it. Furthermore, there is also a particular way of using crystals that can especially target that area of your life. If you are able to properly match your crystals with the facet of your life that you are intending to heal, then you will be well on your way to constructing an effective healing practice. In this chapter, I will go through some of the most common areas in which people heal themselves using crystals and explain some of the fundamental aspects of that practice.

Anxiety

One of the most common reasons many people will turn to practices like crystal healing and meditation is stress. Nowadays, many people live very stressful lives, so practices like these are all the more necessary. Crystals regulate the body's natural rhythms, which is ideal for anxiety sufferers. Because anxiety is all about speeding up our rhythms to create a high-stress body, regulating our vibrations is essential. Amethyst, tiger's eye, and aquamarine are three of the most commonly used crystals for anxiety. In terms of methods, many people will either meditate with these crystals when they are experiencing immediate anxiety, or they will wear them around when they are experiencing lower-level, constant anxiety. If you follow these methods, your crystals should be able to help you regulate your moods and create a less anxious you!

Change

We all go through changes in our lives, but most of us wish that we could have a little more control over the changes we experience. There are two main ways in which people use crystals for change. One is to cope with changes outside of our control. Things like deaths, divorces, marriages, and births all have a huge impact on our lives, and crystals can help you manage these changes. Angelite is one of the most common stones used for change acceptance. Consider keeping some by your bed at night during transitional periods to help guide you into your new life. The other way people use crystals for change is to manifest change in areas that feel stale. This means that you are trying to bring about new experiences, relationships, and thoughts. For this side of change, you want to use either clear quartz for clarity or malachite for purging negative energy. Both of these crystals will guide you toward a new future worth pursuing. To use these crystals properly, incorporate them into your manifestation or meditation practices so you can be very clear about what you want.

Connection

Forging better connections is one of the things crystals are particularly good at. Similar to change, there are three main ways in which people use crystals for connecting purposes. The first kind is connection with the self. This is usually a building of intuition and a mingling of the conscious and subconscious minds. For this purpose, you should use a crystal such as turquoise to help open yourself up to your innermost desires. Second of all, there are connections with other people, both romantic and platonic. To help boost your ability to communicate, empathize, and care for others, you should choose stones like rose quartz and green jade. Finally, there is a connection with the universe at large or the spiritual world. This means opening yourself up to some of the higher forces that tend to go unnoticed in everyday life. For this purpose, you should choose either amethyst or clear quartz to bring that higher knowledge into your life.

Balance

Creating harmony in your life is one of the most important things to do on your spiritual journey. An unbalanced life can lead to a myriad of problems, including misalignment, confusion, and misdirection of life goals. If you are experiencing a lack of balance in your life, it can be a hard thing to pinpoint. There are a lot of consequences to having a lack of balance, which can reverberate throughout your entire body and every aspect of yourself. For this reason, an imbalance in your body can lead to all kinds of serious complications, such as low confidence, lack of groundedness, and suffering relationships. Thus, bringing balance to your life is essential. If you want a crystal that is good for balance, you should choose either a crown chakra crystal like amethyst or a strong variety of crystals. Creating a wide range of crystals to use in a grid or to wear together can ensure that all your bases are covered and you are able to make certain bodily faculties work in harmony with one another.

Concentration

Concentrating is something a lot of people struggle with, especially those with concentration-based disorders such as obsessive-compulsive disorder (OCD) or attention deficit hyperactivity disorder (ADHD). Issues with concentration can have an effect on your work performance, your interactions with other people, and your creative pursuits. But concentration means more than just your ability to pay attention to something in the moment. Concentration can also mean your level of focus in your life or your ability to choose a lane and commit to things or truly consider what you want to do with your life. People who lack concentration in a major way often switch between jobs frequently, never able to settle on what they like. They might also struggle to maintain long-term relationships because they find themselves overwhelmed by the number of options available to them. In these cases, people might be lacking in direction and purpose, which can leave them feeling really lost in life. For this mental state, you will want crystals that are associated with the third eye chakra and focus in general. Clear quartz, especially in the Vogel cut, is a great place to start. These crystals will help you see past the immediate clutter to the higher purpose you want to have in life.

Grounding

Another thing many people struggle with is feeling grounded. If you are someone who moves around a lot or moved around a lot as a child, you might find that you lack a place that feels like home or where you have roots. Those experiencing cultural diaspora might also feel a lack of groundedness. But it's not just a place that people might feel grounded in. You might have lived in the same place your whole life but don't feel grounded in your relationships or your career. You may feel that these things are not stable and could crumble around you at any moment. Sometimes this lack of feeling grounded results in something called an anxious attachment style, which can cause you to feel constant anxiety over whether you are accepted and loved, unable to truly trust the people in your life to be committed to you. Whether or not a traumatic incident triggered this, you likely feel a lot of pain around this. When using crystals to heal yourself for grounding, you want to get crystals that target your root chakra, such as black tourmaline or black onyx. These crystals will help you start to gain a more grounded perspective on your life and self and settle into where you are.

Conclusion

Crystals reaped their vibrations from the very core of the earth. Coincidentally, we share these vibrations. At our cores, we are made from the same substance and share a profound connection with the earth and thus crystals. Crystals are the way we connect to those core vibrations from whence we came, creating a strong relationship with the earth. It's no wonder, then, that crystals can have such a strong influence over us. We respond to them on a very deep level, recognizing that core connection and allowing it to influence us. There are many spheres of life in which crystals can influence us. They can help us connect with our sense of self, our purpose in life, others' feelings, and the universe at large. They can bring clarity to our life, helping us see through the debris of everyday life. They can create a more balanced mind and body that acknowledges the inherent connection between all the faculties. If we can let in the power of crystals, we are able to heal many aspects of our lives in a deep, long-lasting way.

In this book, I have led you through some of the most fundamental aspects of crystals and their healing practices. First, I showed you the basics of crystal history, helping you to see where the crystal practice comes from and how it has strong roots in many cultures around the world as well as connections to other practices like chakras, meditation, religion, and astrology. Then, I advised you on the ways in which you can purchase your crystals, leading you through all the main options available and listing the pros and cons of each so that you can make an informed decision for yourself. Following that section, we looked at some of the ways in which you can incorporate crystals into your everyday life, such as decorating your home, wearing them, or meditating with them. These purposes can help you to see the many different applications that crystals have, showing you that there are numerous aspects of your life in which crystals can be beneficial. Next, I led you through the processes of taking care of your crystals, from when you first buy them and ongoing maintenance to optimization and storage. This section is incredibly important for crystal users since it reminds you that your crystals are like living things that need to be cared for just like a plant. Finally, I gave you two comprehensive lists: one of some of the most popular crystals out there and the other about some of the facets of life that crystals can help you heal. With these lists, you get a strong sense of the fundamental crystals and their uses, helping you to start to choose which crystals you think are right for you and your intentions with them. After reading, you should now have a basic comprehensive knowledge of crystal healing and should be excited about using crystals going forward!

You now have a window into one of the most powerful healing practices in the world. Many of the ailments and predicaments you have found yourself in over the years can be helped immensely by this crystal practice. Take this knowledge and apply it to your crystal practice, using it to heal your life. After seeing the benefits, you'll wish you had introduced crystals into your life sooner!

Glossary

Amethyst: A purple crystal excellent for balancing.

Angelite: A blue crystal used for purification.

Aura: The vibrations surrounding someone's body.

Black onyx: A black protection crystal corresponding to the root chakra and associated with groundedness.

Black tourmaline: A black purification crystal associated with the root chakra and used for self-help.

Body energy: Natural vibrations that are given off by the body that can be targeted in certain spiritual healing practices.

Chakras: A set of points on the body that correspond to both physical and psychological spheres.

Chi: Core energy of the body that connects the physical and spiritual worlds.

Clear quartz: A clear crystal used for focus.

Cluster crystal: A crystal shape associated with connection.

Crown chakra: The highest chakra on the body, connected to higher knowledge and the spiritual world.

Crystal grid: A method of crystal use that involves placing your crystals in a grid position to bounce their energies off each other.

Cube crystal: A crystal shape that is associated with groundedness.

Fluorite: An aqua-colored crystal associated with clarity.

Green calcite: A green crystal used for trauma healing.

Green jade: A green crystal used for love and connection.

Heart chakra: The chakra at the center of your body, associated with love and connection.

Heart crystal: A crystal shape associated with love and connection, often rose quartz.

Lepidolite: A dark purple crystal used for self-love and confidence.

Malachite: A dark green stone used for radical transformation and growth.

Manifestation: The act of envisioning an event in order to make it happen.

Pointed crystal: A crystal shape used for focus.

Pyramid crystal: A crystal shape associated with desire.

Rose quartz: A type of crystal associated with love and relationships.

Root chakra: The bottom chakra on your body, associated with your sense of self and belonging in the world.

Sacral chakra: The second-lowest chakra on the body, connected to creativity and sexuality.

Smoky quartz: A type of crystal used for banishing negative energy.

Solar plexus chakra: The third chakra on the body, associated with self-esteem and image.

Sphere crystal: A crystal shape associated with greater purpose and connection to the world at large.

Third eye chakra: The sixth chakra on the body and the second from the top, associated with long-term plans and inner truth.

Throat chakra: The fifth chakra on the body, associated with communication and honesty.

Tiger's eye: A type of crystal associated with strong purpose.

Tumbled crystal: A shape of crystal that is very small and portable.

Turquoise: A type of crystal associated with luck.

Vogel crystal: A particular make of crystal created by Marcel Vogel that is cut with specific dimensions to promote focus and clarity.

References

Amethyst meaning: Everything you need to know—Healing properties & every-day uses. (n.d.). Tiny Rituals. https://tinyrituals.co/blogs/tiny-rituals/amethyst-meaning-healing-properties-and-everyday-uses

Ancillette, M. (n.d.). *How to store crystals and gemstones to avoid negative influences.* Angel Grotto. https://angelgrotto.com/crystals-stones/storing/

Avalon, A. (2019, November 3). *Vogel crystals explained.* Avalon InLa'Kesh Blessings & Welcome. https://www.avaloninlakesh.com/vogel-crystals-explained/

A beginner's guide to crystal healing. (n.d.). Therapy Directory. https://www.thera-py-directory.org.uk/blog/2014/01/16/a-beginners-guide-to-crystal-healing

Black onyx meaning: Healing properties, uses, & benefits. (n.d.). Tiny Rituals. https://tinyrituals.co/blogs/tiny-rituals/black-onyx-meaning#:~:text=Black%20Onyx%20is%20a%20root

Carlos, K. (2018). *Crystal healing practices in the Western world and beyond.* https://stars.library.ucf.edu/cgi/viewcontent.cgi?article=1283&context=honorstheses

Chee, C. (2021, September 10). *Angelite: Meaning & healing properties of this blue crystal.* Truly Experiences Blog. https://trulyexperiences.com/blog/angelite-crystal/#:~:text=What%20Chakra%20Is%20Angelite%20Good

Clear quartz crystal: Meaning & healing properties. (2021, September 20). Truly Experiences Blog. https://trulyexperiences.com/blog/clear-quartz/

Crystal shapes. (n.d.). The Australian Museum. https://australian.museum/learn/minerals/what-are-minerals/crystal-shapes/

Crystals 101. (n.d.). Adelphi. https://home.adelphi.edu/~sa21715/Crystals101.html

Crystals for accepting change. (n.d.). Crystal Vaults. https://www.crystalvaults.com/crystal-reference-guide/crystals-for-change/

Ekhart, E. (2021, April 14). *What is Chi?* Ekhart Yoga. https://www.ekhartyoga.com/articles/practice/what-is-chi#:~:text=Chi%20is%20your%20life%20force

Energy reading 101: What your aura colors say about you. (2020, July 19). Mind Body Green. https://www.mindbodygreen.com/articles/aura-colors-and-their-meanings

Enhance your meditation practice with crystals. (2018, July 17). Chopra. https://chopra.com/articles/enhance-your-meditation-practice-with-crystals

Estrada, J. (2019, October 25). *Crystal shapes matter—Here's what they mean and how to amplify their power.* Well+Good. https://www.wellandgood.com/crystal-shapes/

Fluorite meaning: Healing properties & everyday uses. (n.d.). Tiny Rituals. https://tinyrituals.co/blogs/tiny-rituals/fluorite-meaning-healing-properties-everyday-uses

Guhr, A., & Nagler, J. (n.d.). *Crystal healing: The ancient tradition—The therapeutic power, magic and mystery of gems, stones and crystals.* https://www.earthdancer.co.uk/wp-content/uploads/2011/03/aaCrystalpower.pdf

Healing crystals for your home or office. (2021, April 20). Desert USA. https://www.desertusa.com/dusablog/healing-crystals-for-your-home-or-office/

Healing properties and benefits of malachite. (n.d.). Gempundit. https://www.gempundit.com/blog/malachite-stone-uses-meaning-and-healing-properties#:~:text=The%20empowering%20Malachite%20balances%20the

Houston, D. (2018, December 23). *Green-calcite: Meanings, properties and powers.* Crystals and Jewelry. https://meanings.crystalsandjewelry.com/green-calcite/

Houston, D. (2019, May 17). *How to program crystals.* Crystals and Jewelry. https://meanings.crystalsandjewelry.com/how-to-program-crystals/

How to arrange crystals in your home, according to the experts. (n.d.). Eva Gems & Jewels. https://evagemsandjewels.com/blogs/insights/how-to-arrange-crystals-in-your-home

How to charge your crystals. (2020, April 22). C Magazine. https://magazinec.com/beauty/how-to-charge-your-crystals/

How to cleanse, charge, and activate healing crystals. (2022, April 27). Healthline. https://www.healthline.com/health/how-to-cleanse-crystals#using-smaller-stones

How to meditate with chakra stones. (n.d.). Conscious Items. https://consciousitems.com/blogs/practice/how-to-meditate-with-chakra-stones

How to meditate with crystals. (n.d.). Verywell Mind. https://www.verywellmind.com/how-to-meditate-with-crystals-5214020

How to tell if a crystal is real in 7 easy ways. (n.d.). Tiny Rituals. https://tinyrituals.co/blogs/tiny-rituals/hw-to-tell-if-a-crystal-is-real

An introduction to gem identification. (n.d.). International Gem Society. https://www.gemsociety.org/article/how-gems-are-identified/

Lepidolite meaning: Healing properties & everyday use. (n.d.). Tiny Rituals. https://tinyrituals.co/blogs/tiny-rituals/lepidolite-meaning-healing-properties-everyday-use

Mael, M. (2021, October 25). *How often should you cleanse and charge crystals?* Michal & Company. https://michalandcompany.com/how-often-cleanse-and-charge-crystals/

Marcel Vogel and healing crystals. (n.d.). Crystal Light and Sound. https://www.crystallightandsound.com/who-was-marcel-vogel/

Meditating with crystals. (n.d.). Better Sleep. https://www.bettersleep.com/blog/meditating-with-crystals/

Need more courage & motivation in your life? Reach for this powerhouse crystal. (2022, May 30). Mind Body Green. https://www.mindbodygreen.com/articles/tigers-eye#:~:text=Tiger%27s%2Deye%20is%20closely%20related

The one crystal your collection is missing for grounding & protection. (2022, March 12). Mind Body Green. https://www.mindbodygreen.com/articles/black-tourmaline-healing-properties-how-to-use-more#:~:text=Which%20chakra%20is%20associated%20with

Palermo, E. (2017, June 23). *Crystal healing: Stone-cold facts about gemstone treatments.* Live Science. https://www.livescience.com/40347-crystal-healing.html

Regan, S. (2021, June 15). *How to know if your crystals need charging + 9 potent methods.* Mind Body Green. https://www.mindbodygreen.com/articles/how-to-charge-crystals

Roberts, T. (2022a, March 22). *25 of the best crystals for balance and healing.* Sarah Scoop. https://sarahscoop.com/25-of-the-best-crystals-for-balance-and-healing/

Roberts, T. (2022b, March 30). *25 of the best powerful crystals for health & wellness.* Sarah Scoop. https://sarahscoop.com/25-of-the-best-powerful-crystals-for-health-wellness/

Rocha, U. (2017, August 30). *What is an aura and how do crystals help or heal it?* Stonebrick. https://stonebridgeimports.ca/a/500-what-is-an-aura-how-do-crystals-help-or-heal-it

Scoop, S. (2022, June 1). *25 best crystals to use for grounding and healing energy.* Sarah Scoop. https://sarahscoop.com/25-best-crystals-to-use-for-grounding-and-healing-energy/

Seeing aura colors may reveal inner truths. (n.d.). Goodnet. https://www.goodnet.org/articles/seeing-aura-colors-may-reveal-inner-truths

6 tips for buying and using crystals (A beginner's guide). (2014, March 11). Thought Catalog. https://thoughtcatalog.com/claudia-st-clair/2014/03/your-essential-guide-to-buying-and-choosing-crystals/

16 crystals for prosperity & abundance. (n.d.). Tiny Rituals. https://tinyrituals.co/blogs/tiny-rituals/crystals-for-prosperity

Smoky quartz: Meaning & healing properties of this mysterious crystal. (2021, September 10). Truly Experiences Blog. https://trulyexperiences.com/blog/smoky-quartz/

The spiritual science of crystal healing: Chapter 7 working with Vogel. (n.d.). Satya Center. https://www.satyacenter.com/pages/crystal-wisdom-of-marcel-vogel-chapter7

Stelter, G. (2016, October 4). *Chakras: A beginner's guide to the 7 chakras.* Healthline. https://www.healthline.com/health/fitness-exercise/7-chakras#The-takeaway

Stone energy: How to choose a crystal that will rock your world. (n.d.). Cosmic Cuts. https://cosmiccuts.com/blogs/healing-stones-blog/stone-energy-how-to-choose-a-crystal-that-will-rock-your-world

10 healing crystals for concentration and focus. (n.d.). Cosmic Cuts. https://cosmiccuts.com/blogs/healing-stones-blog/healing-crystals-for-concentration-and-focus

3 simple ways to charge crystals with intentions. (n.d.). WikiHow Health. https://www.wikihow.health/Charge-Crystals-with-Intentions

Top 10 reasons why you should wear crystals & gemstone jewellery. (n.d.). Nature's Magick. https://naturesmagick.com.au/blogs/natures-magick-blog/top-10-reasons-why-you-should-wear-crystals-gemstone-jewellery

Turquoise chakras. (n.d.). Durango Silver. https://www.durangosilver.com/turquoise-chakras.html#:~:text=Turquoise%20is%20a%20stone%20of

The 20 best crystals for communication. (n.d.). Tiny Rituals. https://tinyrituals.co/blogs/tiny-rituals/crystals-for-communication

20 healing crystals for anxiety & stress. (n.d.). Tiny Rituals. https://tinyrituals.co/blogs/tiny-rituals/crystals-for-anxiety

Use these 6 crystals to connect with the universe. (2018, April 18). Yoga Journal. https://www.yogajournal.com/yoga-101/use-these-6-crystals-to-connect-with-the-universe/

Using crystals for chakra healing. (2021, May 17). Ohana. https://ohanayoga.com/crystals-for-chakra-healing/

Vogel crystals explained. (2019, November 3). Avalon. https://www.avaloninlakesh.com/vogel-crystals-explained/

What is an authentic Vogel crystal? (n.d.). Crystal Light and Sound. https://www.crystallightandsound.com/what-is-a-vogel-crystal/

Why you need to program your crystals and how. (n.d.). Unique Fengshui. https://uniquefengshui.com/programming-your-crystals/

Your guide to charging crystals with intention. (n.d.). Bustle. https://www.bustle.com/life/how-to-charge-crystals-intention-experts

Made in United States
Troutdale, OR
03/27/2024

18741130R00089